PRICK OF THE SPINDLE

PRINT EDITION | ISSUE 9

MASTHEAD

BOARD OF DIRECTORS

Prick of the Spindle was established in March 2007 as a quarterly online literary journal with a corresponding Kindle Magazine edition (the first literary journal to be available as a Kindle magazine), and is now exclusively a biannual print journal.

Prick of the Spindle recognizes new talent as well as established voices. We are simply looking for well-written, interesting works that are fresh, original, and engaging. We publish poetry, fiction (from flash to novella-length), drama, creative and academic nonfiction, articles, interviews, literary reviews, film, and visual art. Although we do not publish genre fiction, we are open to different forms. These may be more traditional, but infused with freshness and innovation; or experimental but not chaotic: if it is chaos in complete freedom of form you are aiming at, envelop it within some structure, even if only the structure of meaning. To submit, visit www.prickofthespindle.org for the link to the submission manager.

Prick of the Spindle, Inc. is a 501(c)(3) nonprofit organization.

If you are a person or organization interested in advertising, sponsorship, or in making a tax-deductible charitable donation, please contact Cynthia Reeser at pseditor (at) prickofthespindle (dot) com.

Sponsorship levels are as follows:

COUNCIL: $3,000 for acknowledgement in the print journal for 3 years and two lifetime subscriptions.
PATRON: $1,000 for acknowledgement in the print journal for 2 years and a lifetime subscription.
FRIEND: $500 for acknowledgement in the print journal for 1 year and a lifetime subscription.

We welcome contact from publishers who may be seeking reviews of upcoming or recently issued books. All questions should be directed to pseditor (at) prickofthespindle (dot) com.

Postal correspondence may be directed to:

Prick of the Spindle
P.O. Box 170607
Birmingham, AL 35217

ISSN 1940-5499.

CONTENTS

| ISSUE 9 | FALL/WINTER 2015 |

ART

George Davis Cathcart : Illustrations

Cover art: Untitled by George Davis Cathcart

PRICK
OF THE
SPINDLE

| ISSUE 9 |

| FALL/WINTER 2015 |

"Untitled" by George Davis Cathcart

A Conversation with Jason Tandon

Interview by Stephanie Renae Johnson

Quality of Life by Jason Tandon

Black Lawrence Press, Oct. 2013

ISBN: 978-1937854287

Paperback, 55 pp., $14

Jason Tandon was born in Hartford, CT in 1975. He is the author of three collections of poetry: *Quality of Life* (Black Lawrence Press, 2013); *Give over the Heckler and Everyone Gets Hurt* (Black Lawrence Press, 2009), winner of the 2006 St. Lawrence Book Award; and *Wee Hour Martyrdom* (Sunnyoutside, 2008). His work has appeared in *AGNI Online, Boston Review, Esquire, Harvard Review Online, Mid-American Review, Prairie Schooner, Spoon River Poetry*

Review, and on NPR's The Writer's Almanac. He holds a BA and MA in English from Middlebury College and an MA in Writing from the University of New Hampshire, and teaches in the Arts & Sciences Writing Program at Boston University.

Don't let Jason Tandon fool you with his small book of poetry, *Quality of Life*. Though brief, this collection plunges readers into a rendering of life as it really is. I was lucky enough to ask Jason Tandon a couple of questions about the book.

Stephanie Renae Johnson: First of all, I have to applaud you for writing such a wonderful collection. I was fooled at first by how easy your poems are to read, but then, the depth of the poems caught me completely by surprise. It's one of those collections where I think, "Oh, I could write like that," and then sit down and just stare at the page, much like how brilliant dancers make salsa look easy. How long do you spend on a single poem?

Jason Tandon: There was a time when I wanted to be a short story writer, mainly because of Hemingway and Carver. I felt the same way when I read their writing, and of course when I tried to imitate it I failed miserably. But I think I had their work in mind when I was writing *Quality of Life*. I wanted poems that most anyone could read and feel like they could have written, and maybe be surprised that these were poems at all.

It usually takes me several months or years to write a single poem with which I am pleased. In many cases I never seem to finish, or I cheat or give up too readily. The poems have a fluid quality about them; they often remain open to revision. Even when I read them in public I'm making changes.

I've learned, since publishing *Quality of Life*, that my poems are best when they have lain around for at least a year or so. There have been too many times when I have accepted lines and poems too quickly. With this new book, I'm working on resisting that impulse. The challenge is to make poems that are composed from different fragments written from different frames of mind to read with a coherence and kinetic energy.

SRJ: The language is so simple, but so elegant. My favorite example of this is "Love Poem (Redux)": every word is hand-picked. What is your editing process like?

JT: I prefer Dickinson to Whitman. I love the way short poems look on the page, as if the words were brush strokes. One of the difficulties I have writing poems is that the words seem to mar the page. Words ruin the silence, the purest poetic state. Silence is never cliché. Too many words, or words of a certain type, and you have prose. The gaps between the lines, the white spaces, allow for reader participation and imagination to take place; they are a place for readers to associate and dream. I think Bachelard said something like that.

I got a little loose in that regard with *Quality of Life*. I think my poems are most successful when I have taken the eyedropper approach: every word carefully selected, lingered over. Economy and sound are two of my main considerations in revision.

SRJ: I think there's a strong similarity to Billy Collins' voice in your work, both in theme—death, (especially "Later Poem"); life; sex—and in voice. What poets do you find yourself reading and emulating?

JT: There are some poetic principles that Collins believes in that I had in mind when writing these poems. I agreed that readers need reasons to care about your work and those reasons should be pleasure-oriented. I was also aiming for an accessibility of language and subject. Title and opening lines should situate a reader in a stable context and invite them into the poem. At the same time I found myself wanting a little more engagement with trials and tribulations, poems with a little more grit, without the spin-off into some flight of fancy. When I was writing *Quality of Life* I was heavily reading Jane Kenyon, early Gary Soto, early Stephen Dunn, and Robert Bly.

There are, of course, many different audiences and different approaches, and in my new book I am consciously trying different things.

SRJ: I have to ask: your wife was actually the one who queried me for an interview, which is wonderfully different for me. Is she the person you show your poetry first? If not her, who first looks at your work?

JT: She is the only one I show my poems to before I send them out to journals. This is another point in which I am in agreement with Collins. He says somewhere that he is always surprised at some of the acknowledgments in books of poetry, how many people had a hand in the composition. The poems are no longer yours. My wife is a careful reader, a very intelligent person, who had no poetry experience prior to meeting me. For this book, she was my ideal reader. Writing is a solitary practice for me. I sit in a small room at the back of the house with the door closed and I work. I consider the editors of journals my workshop. And their silences speak volumes!

SRJ: After reading your collection, I have to confess: I'm terrified to ever be a parent! You so exquisitely capture the pressure families, parents, and spouses go through. What made you choose this theme in your work?

JT: My last book, *Wee Hour Martyrdom*, was more dream-like with less narrative. In *Quality of Life*, I wanted to create realistic and dramatic situations. I was thinking about subjects that were far away from an academic milieu, more visceral, immediate, common. Work, weddings, divorce. In the poem, "Sugaring," for example, I wrote the line, "I'm sorry I paid such little attention," and I thought, *Can I say that in a poem? Use the word "sorry"?* I started writing more lines in which I just tell things amidst the showing. In "Sugaring," I trusted that many people have probably placed their needs above someone else's, blinded themselves to the sympathy a situation calls for, and if they could see that person again, would apologize, profusely and profoundly.

There's a fine line here: you want to provide enough details and use language freshly so that the poem gives pleasure and is worth re-reading. At the same time, you don't want to bog the reader down in a situation so overly or uniquely described that it can't be anyone else's.

SRJ: As a father (here, I'm assuming, so correct me if I am wrong), but you seem to present this idea of a layered memory: the narrators in your poems remember their own childhood and then filter the childhoods of their children through their own memories. I wonder, how do memories of your childhood affect writing about parenthood for you?

JT: I really don't remember much of my childhood, though I would say I had a very happy and stable one. Again I wanted to give the impression of verisimilitude, as if the "I" is me, and all of this really happened. "On Turning Thirty-Four," for example, was a collage of several fragments. If I detailed the composition of the poem, any effect on the reader would surely dissipate. I was not a father at the time of writing it. I did not have a son. There was no kiddie pool. Stanza three happened to a neighbor of mine. See what just happened?

SRJ: Could you comment more on the line about how you feel you can't apologize in poems? Do you maybe feel like readers won't accept apologies? In addition to this, what do you expect from your readers?

JT: It was the directness of the sentiment that worried me. Sometimes I agree with Hugo's paraphrase of the idea that, without sentiment, there is no risk; other times I want to write poems made purely of images, so that readers can derive their own interpretative possibilities. But this is a difference between painting and poetry: words like "sorry," "love," and "happy" exist in a poet's medium. I understand when editors of journals want me to tell more; I also understand when others want me to show more and trust a reader's intelligence. As far as my readers, I have no expectations. If my poem fails to elicit an emotion, give pleasure, or connect with someone on any level, I'm solely to blame.

A Nebraskan Refrain

Saja Chodosh

The sandhill crane is one of the most conspicuous birds of the prairie region. Every farmer
boy knows its call, and on fair days has seen large flocks soaring at great heights, slowly
passing northward.
—Stephen S. Visher, from "Notes on the Sandhill Crane"

It is because their song carries
by the bruised peach sun,
long ink legs melt
into switch grass, bluestem—
blushed in forgotten moonlight.

because we all want
to be courted
with a dance
in the Platte River:
watershed of love—
swamp bottom, still edge.

because nothing ends
by the water—

each braided current
croons past parched grassland,
grey peaks, and we must
hum meaning yet again—

flushed, dreaming of spring
frost, a tapered cove
of morning song.

THE INVENTION OF MONSTERS / PLAYS FOR THE THEATRE BY C. DYLAN BASSETT

REVIEW BY CYNTHIA REESER

Plays Inverse, 2015

ISBN: 978-0-9914183-2-9

Paperback, 75 pp., $12.95

Poet C. Dylan Bassett, author previously of *Some Futuristic Afternoons* (Strange Cage, 2014) and co-author (with Summer Ellison) of *The Invention of Monsters/A Performance in One Act* (iO Books, 2014), brings together selected prose poems collated as dramatic sketches, separated into four "acts" in *The Invention of Monsters/Plays for the Theatre* (Plays Inverse, 2015). The poems are brief and visual, and all are titled, simply, "[Scene]."

   The Invention of Monsters/Plays for the Theatre is largely concerned with matters of the self:

the outsider, the self within the self, the overlapping aspects of self, the self within others, boundaries and lack thereof, and so on. In the third poem of the first section, which is titled "The Invention of Monsters," the self is never centered in the self, never quite. This "scene" opens with a passing image of a woman and baby, who are intended, mostly, to appear as props. The author writes: "The self occurs but only as proxy," a line that underscores the sense of narrative distance by drawing attention to the dislocality of the speaker/narrative voice. This is distance both between the narrative itself and the voice it employs, as well as distance between that voice and others, like the mother and baby, who appear as characters in the narrative. This is a collection that plays at being a play, each piece being a scene, but only touches on these dramaturgical leanings, never fully engaging with the format: but! this is intentional. The format itself is a play by proxy, as uncentered in or unknowing of itself as, the author seems to be saying, any of us are (un)centered within ourselves, our knowledge and understanding of ourselves, our groundedness in our own lives.

The next poems are a continuing dialogue of the question of identity, the question of the self, and speak to the fluidity of "I":

Now that I'm here I could be anyone. (Carnivorous I. I of the graven image.) The role of the boy is played by a skeleton inside a smaller boy. The old woman is played by a younger woman with white hair. Wind is defined as a crooked line, a voice of various proportions. Birds explode into smaller birds.

These birds exploding are the pieces of identity, the fragmented self or personality/ies. In the excerpt above, now we are getting to actual scene, the delineations of characters on a stage, where the previous pieces have been setting the tone and therefore function more like stage directions. The idea not only of fragmented and fluid identity, but also nested identity, also lives here: the skeleton inside the boy, the younger woman within the older. Don't we all carry pieces of our former selves within us, our 8-year-old selves nested somewhere within our present selves? Within every old woman is the memory of the girl she used to be, the author seems to be saying, within every young man his younger self. Other poems in the same section continue the dialogue: "I am the tiny person inside my skull. One of us sees the other through a window." For all the world's a stage, and we merely players within it; and we are players on the stages of our own lives as well, players within our own minds: the ego recognizing the id. And on our stages, we are actors moving among roles, donning and doffing identities:

> I pretend myself back to life. I put on the correct suit and feel the correct feeling. [...] So much meat, so much clothing. The landscape and the language are the same sensory derangement. Loosely a fox hatches from a chicken egg.

Not only is the self questioned, but the stage as well: that is, our individual realities, reality as we know it. With the right amount of sensory derangement, or biological tampering, for that matter, could there not be a reality in which a fox hatches from an egg? On the stage, with its false lights and trickeries of makeup and shadow and costume, anything is possible; any reality can congeal. But this line speaks not only to perception and reality, but also to incongruity: something completely other emerges from another thing, rather than what is expected—which sounds a lot like the creative process. Perhaps more to the point, this incongruity seems to imply the cognitive dissonance that people often feel when questioning the identity. There is much here of gender identity, much of mirroring ("My face is a mirror, other faces come and go."). We reflect one another, the identities we choose to wear; we are influenced by others and they by us. Hence, we are all mirrors to one another. We walk, ever, in halls of mirrors and call this our reality.

The next section, "Fantasies about Cowboys," pushes into this idea, continues the dialogue about identity constructs and perception: "I'm only shaped like a man. The eye holds prisoner what it beholds. Seeing a hole in the ground, I see myself." We are beings who trap beauty, who put pretty birds in cages to behold at whim. It is a subtle way of consuming that beauty, attempting to take it into ourselves, to become it in some way, if only through the keeping of it within the perception, the mind. Actors take on the identity of the roles they play, and, "When the actors remove their clothing, we cannot remember whom to pity, whom to blame." We all are wearing costumes; when the businessman puts on his suit and goes to work, he becomes a businessman; this may be quite a different person from the same man who wears shorts on the weekend—we all have different identities for different occasions.

The third section, "Scenes of Heroism," is largely concerned with war. There are images of literal war, and beneath the surface of that lies the war with the self, id at war with ego, self at war with self, self against others:

> The morning struggles to assert itself. The rifle takes its aim. The dim crow dissolves into the eye of the cat. [...] A painter paints herself out of the landscape. Nowhere is the past. Even more broken glass.

We see in this, too, erasure: the painter does not include herself in her work, just as the author (usually) remains invisible to the reader. But this is not that. The author of *The Invention of*

Monsters, while not visible, hovers at the periphery of our awareness as readers, for we are reading his words regarding self and what it is, and we cannot help but think of the self/id/ego that developed this construct, that holds up this mirror in which we can view ourselves. We can redefine ourselves and shape our realities as we wish, but sometimes, to do that, there is a cost, "even more broken glass."

The next section, "A Tent for the Night," deals, on the main, with religion. Herein lie nested identities, searching for some meaning greater than themselves:

> Some men and some women made in the image of God. In part this is because many people are content with existing reciprocity. The wet bird flicks past, the hand has waved. God walks into a man and a baby goes to sleep. The hunter shoots the deer over and over, but the deer won't die. Look at anything long enough and you begin to imitate it. To love something you must carry it on your back.

The tent that is the namesake of this section I interpret to mean religion, which is, to many, a comforting blanket of protection, much like the protective casing of the body around the soul. If the baby goes to sleep when "God walks into a man," then the comfort of religion and faith, the poet seems to be saying, pacifies the childish things of the younger self within the self, helps it to grow up, succors the primal id so that it may rest, so that it may find peace.

And who is the monster of the book's namesake? It is, of course, ourselves. Any one of us can put on a suit and go out into the world, perfectly respectable; any one of us is capable of transformation, not only exterior (like changing clothes), but interior as well. It is our interiority and the interior life—the life of the mind, beliefs, our understanding of ourselves, our points of view toward things such as war and religion—that make us who we are. C. Dylan Bassett has created an ever-evolving dialogue about the nature of identity in *The Invention of Monsters/Plays for the Theatre*. In the creation of this dialogue and its exploration, the author is quite successful, not only for his often impressive use of language and imagery, but for the way he uses that language to plumb the depths of his subject matter.

Dented Silver Trumpet

Caleb Nelson

This is not the story of my father,
waterlogged in the basement,

trapped with blue wrenches in his hands,
equations rising

from his choking mouth. This
is not the silence of feathers

in a crown-white grove,
turtle-green sea. We

face each other like broken shells
beneath the furnace.

KEEPING ME STILL BY RENEE EMERSON

REVIEW BY CYNTHIA REESER

Winter Goose Publishing, 2014

ISBN: 978-1-941058-11-4

Paperback, 78 pp., $10.60

Author of three previous chapbooks, Renee Emerson released her first full-length poetry collection, *Keeping Me Still*, from Winter Goose Publishing in 2014, the reading of which Robert Pinsky praised as resembling "the pleasure of watching a gifted athlete." Reading through the collection, it is easy to see why he dubs her "a swift, muscular *noticer*"; the poet's vision is one that connects the self, the body, awareness and perception, to the world around as though the delineation between the two is no more incidental than a "thin sheet of ice" ("In

Keeping"). Right away, there are polarizations: self/not-self, male/female, born/unborn. But these are not simply black-and-white modes of opposing forces; the significance lies in how these forces come together or forge bonds to create another thing altogether new, how they transform and give over to change.

Section I deals largely with babies and children. "When We Started Trying" calls to our attention what happens in autumn: "the orderly growth of summer has collapsed." But not only this:

> Maples become book margins, white
>
> spider limbs from some lightless place.
> I speculate my body: graveyard, indefinite
>
> wintering, or apricot sweetness.

In the midst of this striving for new life, the body is a graveyard; the lush growth of summer gives way to autumn, a time preceding the frozen gestation of winter. The body is barren for a time, but seasons change. The polarizations are not so black and white that they are opposites, but merely points on an ever-turning wheel, all connected to the other: death gives way to barrenness, which makes way for fertilization and gestation, and the wheel keeps turning. And in this, there is an order. Emerson's poetry has a great deal to do with order, or the desire for it, the constant and very human striving toward it.

The line, not the poetic line, but the concept of line and that which is linear, is a recurring image in Emerson's work. "Ascension" has "a line of geese"; in another poem, "A Pleading Sound" (first published in *Prick of the Spindle* Online Edition, Vol. 6.3), "You could / just hear [the coyotes] over the straight-line winds / that scythed the fields"; there is also the telling line of a pregnancy test ("A Thin Blue Line"). Other times, the line is disrupted, as with the "broken arrow" and "dotted line" in "When We Started Trying." The line appears most often in connection with a reaching out, as with the couple trying to conceive, or with a receding, as with the field that connects the people safe in their homes with the threat of danger that lies just beyond.

There is the seen and the unseen, and the line that reaches between the two is more of a border or boundary: the mother hears the heartbeat of her unborn child, but cannot see the child or touch her yet; she is a thing to be protected. Contrast this with the heard howls of the coyotes beyond the field, who cannot be seen but are a thing to be kept at bay, a thing to be feared and to hide from, safe within the home. In "Safekeeping," the line becomes curved, more delicate: "Brimming, divided heartbeats like misplaced commas / sectioning the lace of my insides." Here, the child is kept safely within the mother's womb. In "Keep," the child does not survive outside the womb:

> The safest place in a stronghold
> is called a "keep." Not viable,
>
> they labeled her. The mother could not
> keep.

The idea of *keeping* is a major theme in *Keeping Me Still*. The word appears in many of the poems' titles in various forms. Being that the book is largely concerned with family and children, it seems apt: the word calls to mind a castle keep, the fortified tower surrounded by walls; in other words, the home, which is like a womb. It is protection—that of mother, family, and even the body.

Section II moves into ideas of familial bonds, especially those of sisters, and of mother and child. Here, the idea of polarity surfaces again, and the previous theme is reinforced: "there are no two things in this world / that are opposite" ("Close to One Another"). In this section also, we find the namesake for the book's title in the poem, "Rachel Takes Vows" (hearkening to the Biblical story of the sisters, Leah and Rachel):

> I remember once Mother wrapping brownies in a paper towel, setting them on the dresser's yellow corner, and I grabbed a bite and she'd said *do you need that?* And I felt big, not volleyball off-season big but actual big, like a body in the suit of a body, and then I skip dinner because where am I heading with all this tasting? So terrifying to grow, let me get small like a bird that can be cupped in your hands, a goose under your arm, all day your arm around me, keeping me still.

Here, the word *keeping* is used to imply restraint and protection; its use in this poem speaks to security and the need to feel safe in order to have self-control. Beyond that, it is finding a sense of completeness, wholeness, and satisfaction or fulfillment in the self with the turning away of superficial need. Contrast this with the acute, physical need of a child, and we find another polarity. The idea of need is further explored in Section III, where the poet writes of hunger and desire ("The Peach and the Pit") and of the desire for desire ("Ravenous").

Looking beyond thematic considerations, Emerson's use of language is notable. For instance, she writes in "Leah Plays for Keeps" of her burgeoning pregnancy: "The summer we were twenty-five, we swam / every day, my expanding belly more magnificent / wrapped in the gossip of a spandex swimsuit." It is not only the poet's striking and vivid use of language and thematic elements, but also of imagery that knit the poems in this collection together to make it such a strong debut. "The Way It Holds You" is a fine example of this, for it is as intricately woven as the spider web it describes:

Eight months pregnant,
I hang a clothesline in the back lawn.
In the nursery window, a garden spider
embraces its tightwoven prey. Anonymous
in gauze-white. Moth, horsefly,
creature that thought it had given
wide berth the arcing legs,
the center-poised X. They become husk.
My clothespins like the barn swallows,
solemn, well-spaced
on the wire between our home
and the distant, unseen next.

This poem brings together the primary thematic elements of the collection, and in that sense functions as the centerpiece of the web that is this collection. There is the clothesline and the wire, which call to mind the imagery of line, and here, function as borders, both literal and figurative, something delineating the seen and the unseen. The crossing in the spider's web symbolizes the unknown, in a departure from the order that the straight line signifies. Here, as with the previous poems in the collection, the line is not broken, but crossed, catching something and keeping it. There is also the keep of the cocoon of the spider's prey, to be compared with the cocoon of the womb; both will eventually become empty husks, but one holds life and the other, death.

It is no surprise that Emerson won the Academy of American Poets Prize (2009), for she has an exceptional collection in *Keeping Me Still*. It is one to be treasured and re-read, and I look forward to her next work.

DISTANCE

PATRICIA COLLEEN MURPHY

"Do you not hear me calling, white deer with no horns?
I have been changed to a hound with one red ear."
—W. B. Yeats

Imagine you are reading this poem at the bottom of a ravine.
Think about its epigraph. How does it apply to you, there?

This poem is supposed to pose a question then answer it.
This poem wants to know how you react to a person

who is over-reacting. This poem is lying
on your lap as you sit on a rock near the stream.

The sun is falling so a shadow spreads over you like a stain.
To read the poem, you must now hold it close to your face.

You, the white deer with no horns. Me, the hound with one red ear.
I am parting the curtains, rubbing a see-circle onto a foggy window.

I am going to send the crows to explain what I mean.

THE STAKED PLAINS BY STEFAN KIESBYE

REVIEW BY CYNTHIA REESER

Saddle Road Press, Nov. 2015

ISBN: 978-0-9913952-7-9

Paperback, 170 pp., $15

The Staked Plains is Stefan Kiesbye's fifth novel, releasing this November from Saddle Road Press. Where Kiesbye's previous books contain more of the noir, *The Staked Plains* is character-focused and noir hovers at the periphery. The true darkness here is in the characters and their willingness to be ruthless and self-serving, no matter the cost. But what else could be expected in a landscape that is, itself, the epitome of death? Querosa, New

Mexico is a godforsaken land where the economy is dry, there is little of opportunity, and even the water supply is disappearing. It is a place where the only abundance is lack.

Querosa sounds like it should mean something, but its closest Spanish relative is *asqueroso/a*, which means, appropriately for this town, "disgusting." Jenny is a new arrival to Querosa and, being that she is coming from Los Angeles, we feel sorry for her, living in such a place. The author strikes up a note of empathy for Jenny's character right away. From the book's opening, we find that "She was a bad psychic when she arrived in Querosa, New Mexico, not because she didn't possess the powers, but because she couldn't control them." Jenny's psychic abilities are linked to the Old World, which hovers at the fringes throughout the book:

> She might have been Irish but wasn't, and there were rumors spread carefully throughout her family's history that her great-great-great-grandmother had been a witch from the Black Forest who'd barely escaped Germany to the New World. Jenny was rather fond of that cobwebbed tale, mended by each generation of women. They kept it intact, even though their last names changed and tore the women apart.

At odds with the Old World are the precepts of Christianity, ever-present in the book in the form of epigraphs preceding every chapter. The epigraphs are quotes from books of the Bible, including one from the non-canonical book, Enoch. Where the Old World is Black Forest and magick and lush, green mystery, Christianity is desert and plagues of insects and forces with great power and overweening egos. Paganism and Christianity are diametrically opposed, both historically and within this novel, where one cannot survive in the presence of the other. Jenny being in the desert, she is Old World within the domain of Christianity (at one point, she is addressed as "the white witch"). No surprise, then, that it is not long before Jenny discovers a death forming within her, in the form of a teratoma in her abdomen, complete with eyes, teeth, hair, feet, and hands, "as though her womb was trying to assemble a child of its own." Not only Jenny, but everyone, or nearly everyone in the novel seems to live on the fringes. There is the dog-boy, Haag, an abandoned, nonverbal child who eats and drinks with the dogs. Both he and the teratoma are unnatural creatures who are not quite human, existing in the periphery of normalcy.

The Biblical epigraphs hovering in the subtext lend subtle clues and commentary on the developing story. The epigraph to Chapter Four reads:

> Semjâzâ taught enchantments, and root-cuttings, ʻArmârôs the resolving of enchantments, Barâqîjâl astrology, Kôkabêl the constellations, Êzêqêêl the knowledge of the clouds, Araqiêl the signs of the earth, Shamsiêl the signs of the sun, and Sariêl the course of the moon. And as men perished, they cried, and their cry went up to heaven...

This excerpt is from the non-canonical Biblical gospel, Enoch 1, which describes (among other things) a group of angels who fell and taught to humans the ways of witchcraft, i.e., enchantments, how to use plants for healing and other purposes (root-cuttings), understanding of the stars, the moon cycles, and weather patterns. Enter Jenny and her great-great-great-grandmother. There is much here in the subtext that functions at a level beyond the residents of Querosa and their attempts to survive in the ruthless landscape and dying economy of the desert.

If Jenny represents Old World paganism, it is J. D. Hartt who represents Christianity. Hartt is the wealthiest, and therefore the most powerful, resident of Querosa, a big fish in a small pond. It is ironic—and maybe fated, given what the characters represent—that Jenny lusts after him. But what she really desires is not the man himself, but his power: "She wanted more than Carl [her husband] was or might ever be. And J. D.'s ruthlessness pleased her." His ruthlessness stems in part from the lack of fear that people in positions of power often have. With J. D. in her life, "Now she had the real thing, the maelstrom, the taste of candy and booze and white powder. She didn't want to confess, and she didn't want to explain." The choice of the word *confess* is interesting, along with the fact Jenny has no desire to do it, and why would she? Confession is, after all, for Christians.

The story and the subtext of *The Staked Plains* is woven with supreme skill and dexterity. The prose is often breathless:

> Garrett [J. D.'s son] would move to Italy and she would be free to openly belong to her new lover. She felt possessed. She was hungry for cold cuts. She could hear the dogs outside the window greeting the boy in the Superman shirt in hushed voices.

As it progresses, this unlikely, always-surprising story of a psychic who reads, not palms, but feet, has the feel of something inevitable hurtling forward toward its destiny—the fatedness of a snowball rolling down a hill, or a falling rock that begins an avalanche. All the pieces fall into place quickly, and while nothing is ever expected, when it does happen, it feels as if it were meant to be that way all along. Beneath a story that begins quietly is a growing sense of disquiet, holes torn in lace curtains to reveal an unsettling tableau, "the distinct feeling of looking at a quiet painting covering an original of far more disturbing content."

PARSE

NATALIE SHARP

I'm worried
I'm not going to know it when I see it,
won't feel its rhizomatic grasping
parsing marrow from bone, or else
its taut skin slipping inside mine
some weekday morning while I inhale
hot gasps of tea across the room
from the idea of someone
I could love.
I want assurance that it will be
nothing like and fully like
my mother always said—the sort that leaves you
half in the breast of the living,
half at the feet of the dead.

The Death of Doorknobs

Jim Gustafson

After "Foreclosure," a work of art by Leila Mesdaghi

I have found the place doorknobs go to die.
They hang themselves on wires. Their plated brass
bodies scratch the air amid the wakes of people
who swing by, quietly like well-oiled hinges.
Doorknobs are relatives of all for whom death comes
through the keyholes of open eyes. They hold hands
open to greet guests, as furnace fans blast winter away
in the vestibule of smiles. At times they cannot handle,
they clutch their fists, slam the frame cold in flames
of frozen words. Knobs themselves outlast their doors,
live past lost keys and remodeled rooms,
until the day they wrap themselves in wire
to sway unlatched in remembrance.

"Untitled" by George Davis Cathcart

LUNULA

RUDY KOSHAR

The day I smashed my thumb in the driver's side door of a '62 Olds Dynamic 88 hardtop, the Four Tops' "I Can't Help Myself" was a big hit. It played on WLS from Chicago almost every hour. It was on the radio as Jimmy Smith steered the Olds two-door into the right-hand bay of the Sunoco gas station. Singing the lines, "Sugar Pie, Honeybunch"—which made me think of Natalie—Jimmy danced before getting to the job. He wasn't much of a dancer. More like a linebacker in a ballet. My asparagus-stalk body had better moves on the dance floor than his big hulk did. But he did something I'd appreciate years later. He performed a kind of moonwalk—heavy, gliding, ghostly, but still a moonwalk—right there on the concrete floor of a station in small-town Michigan. He did a moonwalk before Michael Jackson made it famous. When the song was over, Jimmy stretched his arms over his head. He brought them forward and, holding them chest-high, pressed his hands together so that his biceps rippled. I'd seen biceps like that only in the "Charles Atlas" ads in the car magazines I looked at from time to time. The short sleeves of his blue Sunoco shirt were ready to explode. I wondered then why Jimmy, six inches taller than me, didn't just call me "Benny" instead of "Benjamin."

Jimmy started with an engine wash. It was dirty work, toxic as hell, and I could see greenish-black iridescent slime streaming off the greasy engine and down into the floor drain to who-knew-where. Maybe it was piped into the sluggish St. Joseph River, because those were the days when we dumped used batteries and oil directly into the ravine a mile from the station. Jimmy had me hose down the engine once he sprayed it with whatever radioactive substance he used. Some of the cleaning gunk splattered and I felt a burning sensation on my hands and forearms. My right hand would burn a lot more once I slammed the door on it, but that wouldn't happen for another forty-five minutes.

Once the engine looked almost new, Jimmy dove into the interior. He told me to clean the inside of the windows while he vacuumed the floors and upholstery. He was like a mad anteater when he vacuumed, as if he had a grudge against every splotch of dirt, every French fry under the front seats, every cookie crumb left by some kid who didn't understand that the cleanliness of a man's car was a reflection of his being. He was Patton against Hitler, relentless in his struggle against dirt's reign of terror. He was as profane as Patton too. He muttered "God damn it!" when he jammed his big knuckles feeling under the driver's seat for loose change. He spit out "fuck!" several times when he vacuumed under the steering wheel, always the dirtiest spot in the interior, even if the owner placed the floor mats just so. It was the hardest spot to reach for a big man like Jimmy.

The green carpet on this car was so soiled that Jimmy resorted to the flowery-smelling pink cleaning agent Sunoco gave its stations. It came in an unmarked plastic spray bottle, which Jimmy wielded like a gardener spraying a prize orchid. He made a small spritz under the brake pedal, then up in the right corner, where the driver's shoe always scuffed the carpeted transmission tunnel. Once he had the dirt out, he was careful that the scrubbed section's nap matched the rest of the carpet.

Meanwhile, I sprayed vinyl conditioner on the light green dash and console. Jimmy liked the vinyl to shine like new; no streaks or splotches. I knew that when we drove the car out into the sunlight, Jimmy would get in the back seat and look at the dash from a distance to see if the shine was uniform. He wanted perspective, like a Monet or a Feininger. He wanted to see if the transformative effect he'd been looking for had been achieved. Then he'd get into the front seat to check all the dashboard controls for dust or fingerprints. Those controls had to look pristine, as if no human hand had ever touched them. Virginal. Several times that summer, he'd made me redo the job, which irked me. But once I got to be a veteran of the detailing wars, I understood what Jimmy wanted, and his satisfaction became my only goal. I found that polishing the dashboard, working the dampened rag into the crevices around the speedometer, dusting each button on the radio, had a surprisingly calming effect on me.

Jimmy was in his early thirties and the best auto detailer in Benton Harbor, maybe in Michigan. It was mid-August 1966, and he worked at my father's gas station on the corner of Fair and Britain, in a neighborhood where most folks went to the African Methodist church and music by James Brown, Wilson Pickett, and The Supremes blared from open doors and windows on simmering summer nights. Jimmy's full name was James Elijah Smith. When his friends stopped by the station to shoot the breeze they called him "James," and I heard his mother call him that when she stopped in to get gas for her ancient, impeccably clean Buick. But we at the Sunoco called him "Jimmy," and maybe we were the only ones on the planet who did that.

My father thought it would be good for me, a junior in high school, to learn the gas station business. He figured that soon, I'd escape St. Joseph, a snooty, chalk-white little town across the river from mostly black Benton Harbor. I'd want to go to college, and he knew I could because he always told me, "study hard," which I did. I was the class salutatorian when I graduated, which was funny, because I didn't know there was such a thing until they said, "you're it." But I was weak, my father thought, too bookish, too lost in ideas and daydreams, and so waiting on cars, doing oil changes, repairing flat tires, and working with Jimmy washing and waxing cars—all that would help me learn about "the real world" before I took up with the hippies and braless women at the university in East Lansing.

When the Olds' door mangled my thumb, I was still getting over the night before, when my steady girl Natalie told me she wanted to date around. Things were too serious between us, she said, my hands were roving too freely, it was time to cool it. Maybe that was why my brain froze every few minutes when I was working with Jimmy—Natalie had put me in cold storage—and the door-slamming event happened during one of my personal little Ice Ages. I didn't break the thumb, but the accident left an ugly blue-black-purple nail that disappeared only after a new nail grew in its place.

The day we detailed the Olds was a typical late summer afternoon in Michigan, a high temperature predicted in the mid-80s, with the humidity pressing so hard on the asphalt drive it seemed the earth couldn't withstand the weight. At the pumps, where the cheapest grade of Sunoco "custom-blended" gasoline cost only twenty-nine cents a gallon, you saw toxic fumes create mirage-like waves in the air when you filled up a customer's tank. In the garage bay, in contrast, we had shade and cool water in abundance. An oasis. But even in the cool garage, Jimmy perspired. There were dark stains in the underarms of his blue Sunoco shirt and on his back. He repeatedly wiped his glistening brow with his forearm as he worked. My goal at first was to sweat as much as Jimmy did, to show how hard I was working, but I never could.

"Hey, Benjamin," Jimmy said after we finished the interior. "Get us two pops, okay?"

We leaned against the counter that ran the length of the garage at the back. I sipped on a Nehi grape and Jimmy had the orange drink. We talked. These conversations were important to me. At a time when music, clothes, film, television—the very air young people breathed—questioned Authority, it was interesting for me to get a view of Authority from someone like Jimmy. And since the closest Authority was my old man, whom Jimmy and everyone else at the Sunoco called Boss Man, I had a personal investment in the matter. Not that Jimmy was going to be completely open with me. I wasn't so naïve to expect that.

I knew that Jimmy's parents had come north from Mississippi in World War II seeking jobs in the factories in the Twin Cities, which is how everyone referred to St. Joseph and Benton Harbor in southwestern Michigan, two towns that were as similar as Mussolini and Gandhi. His grandparents were sharecroppers. Jimmy had barely gotten a ninth-grade education. I was about six when I first met him. He stuck in my mind because he was so tall and dark and his name reminded me of Jiminy Cricket, a special culture hero of mine at that age. My father had taken him on as his "wash boy" when he was a teenager. After a while, he'd worked his way up so that he waited on customers out on the drive and helped the mechanic, Hal, with tune-ups and brake jobs. But he made auto detailing his specialty, and my father made plenty of money charging people extra for regular oil changes because he threw in a wash job. For an additional charge, you could get your car expertly detailed. By the time Jimmy was in his early twenties, the station had cars lined up waiting to be serviced, and soon people couldn't come in anymore whenever they felt like it; they had to make an appointment. I liked to hang around the station when I was ten or eleven, just watching what the guys did, helping my dad stack shiny blue and yellow oil cans or put up advertising posters in the little waiting room.

Then Jimmy disappeared, at least from my life. By the time I was in my early teens I'd discovered the Beatles and James Bond novels, and above all, girls. I didn't want to hang around the station any more, and on the rare occasions when I did visit the Sunoco, Jimmy was nowhere to be seen. I asked my father one evening what happened to him.

"He stabbed me in the back," said my father gruffly.

"How?"

"Went off and got a factory job."

"What's wrong with that?" I said, not knowing I'd entered into a minefield and was in imminent danger of having a leg or arm blown off.

"He joined a union."

I learned that evening this was one of the most damning things my father could say about a man. He joined a union. Raised on a fruit farm in small-town Michigan—a war vet who fought in Europe to preserve the freedom *not* to have things like unions, which he associated with socialism, which he thought was the same thing as fascism; a small businessman who assumed that as long as the guy in charge treated everyone fairly, there was no need for workers to join unions—my father said he'd never forgive Jimmy.

"After everything I'd done for him," he said, throwing the newspaper on the floor and looking me in the eye. "Hell, he hardly had a pot to shit in when he came into the station asking for work one afternoon. I gave him a chance. And look what he does. Some of these union guys got to him.

They came into the station, driving nice cars, talking to Jimmy. They turned his head, they did. Told him he'd get better hours and higher pay at the factory as a union man. Didn't tell him how high the union dues were, you can bet on that."

At the tender age of fifteen, I knew there was something radically wrong with my father's view. I'd lived on the white side of the river but I knew about Benton Harbor, and not only because that's where the station was. I knew there were kids my age for whom words like "hope" and "opportunity" were as rare as winning lottery tickets. I saw the desperate cars come into the gas station so packed with people that children were almost falling out of the windows and the woman driving the car would buy just fifty cents of gas and not have the oil or tires checked. I cringed every time Hal blurted out "nigger" and "darkie," which he did a lot, even in front of Jimmy, who'd just laugh and do his work. I'd heard about the freedom riders down South and Martin Luther King and the Civil Rights Act in Mrs. Tilleson's high school social studies class. I sensed that poor people, workers, anyone without power, needed protection of some kind.

Yet I didn't say a thing. It wasn't only that I was scared to speak up against my father. In a way, he was right: I was weak. But I was also with Natalie by that time, and she was more than enough to keep me occupied. The other things—civil rights, Vietnam, the protests, JFK's assassination—still didn't "resonate" for me, as I would say later. I wanted to know more about the larger world but the world hadn't gotten into my bones. Unlike Natalie, who had seeped into every part of my overwrought, reedy self. Why get in a big fight with my father over all that when I could nod, bundle up, pick up my ice skates, and walk two blocks to Whittlesey Rink, where I'd skate with Natalie until nine, and afterwards we'd sit in the warming house while most people left for the night, and maybe we'd have a last hot chocolate from the concession and even a few kisses before they flashed the lights for closing?

The May before we washed the '62 Olds, Jimmy came back to work at the Sunoco, or, as my father told it, he "came crawlin' back from his union pals after the factory laid his sorry ass off." I didn't know what the true story was and I didn't ask—until the day we stood sipping our Nehi grape and orange drinks. Maybe it was the camaraderie I'd built with him (or thought I'd built) since starting work at the station. Or maybe I needed something to take my mind off Natalie.

"Sure is good to learn all this stuff about auto detailing, Jimmy," I said while the WLS newsman reported the latest developments in the Richard Speck mass murder case. "When I have my own car, I'm going to keep it like you taught me."

Jimmy grinned. "Why don't you get the Boss Man to buy you a used car? You'd look sharp sportin' around with that girlfriend a' yours next to you."

"Nope, he wouldn't do that. He wants me to earn the money for something like that."

"Well, he's right, ya know? Your daddy's a smart man. He's worked real hard to get where he is. A good example for you, Benjamin."

"You like working for my dad, Jimmy?"

Jimmy seemed momentarily perplexed by my question. A frown came over his face. He paused as I tipped my Nehi bottle up to get the last sweet gulps of grape pop. The newscaster was finishing up the story about the mixed-up man with a "Born to Raise Hell" tattoo who tortured, raped, and killed eight student nurses from South Chicago Community Hospital on a single night no more than a month before.

"One crazy fucker, he musta been," said Jimmy, shaking his head. I nodded in agreement.

"I wouldn't a' come back if I didn't like workin' for the Boss Man," he said after another long pause.

"But I thought maybe you were never coming back. After what my dad said…"

"'Bout the union?" says Jimmy.

"Yeah."

"The Boss Man was *powerful* mad," said Jimmy. He took his last swig of orange drink, took my bottle, walked over to the pop machine to place both bottles in the wooden crate the Nehi guy would pick up on his weekly delivery route. He came back and smiled at me. "I'd rather work for a man who looks me in the eyes, tells me what he's thinkin'. Ain't nothin' worse than workin' for a man who don't give a man the straight news, you know? I never met the man who owned the factory. I met my foreman, sure, but shit, he didn't give a damn, not even when they laid me off. Not like your pops."

"But he made you start from the bottom again," I said. "You're washing cars and I get to wait on customers and help Hal with oil changes, besides working with you. He demoted you, and you'd worked for him for so long."

"I ain't sayin' I agree with the Boss Man," said Jimmy as he pulled clean rags from a shelf under the workbench. "An' I ain't sayin' the union's a bad thing. Fact is, we need strong unions, now more than ever. Jus' sayin' I know how he feels. How he sees things. I'm jus' sayin' I know I'm workin' for a man who sweats and curses and gets pissed off like I do."

Jimmy turned away and walked toward the center of the garage between the two bays, where an air hose, a grease gun, and a water hose hung from housings attached to the ceiling. He'd tied the water hose in a loop so as not to get tangled in it while we worked. It was time to wet down the exterior of the Olds, so he undid the loop and let the hose hang at full length, where it almost touched the floor. I walked over to him and he handed me the end of the hose without a word.

The Olds' color was Surf-Green Magic-Mirror. Who came up with these names? To me it looked like tired metallic green. But not to Jimmy. Years later, I saw a photo of the sculptor Brancusi eying a mockup of his elegant *Bird in Space*. The photographer captured the sculptor's mixed feelings—enthusiasm, love, a powerful critical edge, including self-criticism. That's how Jimmy looked as he walked around the '62 Olds, considering it from every angle, deciding on his approach, as I sprayed cool water over the green finish.

We used soapy wash mitts to get the dust and grime off the surface. For the rocker panels, which always had caked-on residue that the mitts never removed on their own, Jimmy had me use a sponge encased in finely abrasive plastic netting. Except for tar spots, that sponge removed all the surface dirt on the panels. It was also good for removing bug spots from the headlights, hood, grill, windshield, and side mirrors. I hated this part of the job most of all, and I knew Jimmy could be a cruel taskmaster when it came to removing all the red, yellow, and brown splatters of insect gunk. We'd wax the car a few minutes later, and he didn't want to wax over grit; the surface had to be as clean and smooth as possible. It had to be, as Jimmy said, "as slippery as snot on a doorknob."

As I rinsed the soapsuds off the Olds, Jimmy dampened two chamois to make them supple. He then fed them through a hand-operated wringer on the rusty old washing machine he kept in a corner of the wash bay. He handed me one and then began to dry the car with the other. Jimmy didn't just wield the chamois—he *became* it. After it was soaked and he'd wrung it through the dryer again, he snapped it with a theatrical gesture, as if he were a magician producing a pigeon from a big magenta scarf. No one worked the skin like he did, sliding it across the green paint, wringing, sliding again until no water spots or streaks could be seen. My movements were mechanical and stiff. But Jimmy flowed with the water beading up on the car's surface.

Next came the wax. We always used Meguiar's, which Jimmy insisted on over my father's initial protests. My dad had thought the cheap wax Sunoco supplied was fine. But Jimmy wouldn't take no for an answer. He had to have the good stuff, and my father, being a businessman, saw the logic when the cars lined up for Jimmy's detailing. The money he was bringing in more than made up for using expensive car wax.

We covered every corner of the car, not forgetting the rocker panels, inside and out, or the interior surfaces of the doorframes. Jimmy taught me this area of the car was too often neglected. It was impressive to open up a car door and see the doorframes shine, said Jimmy. It made you feel like you're stepping into someone's clean home.

I slathered wax on the inside frame of the driver's side door. For some reason I decided to slam the door before moving to the other side, and it was then that I smashed my finger. I let out a sharp yelp; then the dizziness came. Jimmy said "Jesus!" and rushed to my side. I felt punch-drunk. He led me by the arm into the back office next to the left-hand bay and sat me down. The office was hidden from the customers who waited out front when their cars were serviced. There was no one else in the garage. Hal was out on the drive waiting on a car and my father was at the auto parts store to pick up a muffler for an exhaust job later that afternoon. My head spun and I felt like throwing up.

"You jus' sit some," said Jimmy softly. He looked at my finger, shook his head, then turned quickly to leave. In a few minutes he was back with a plastic bag full of ice cubes from the Rusty Pig Bar-B-Q next door. They had the best ribs in town, Jimmy always said, maybe the best in southwestern Michigan, but they also had plenty of ice. He wrapped the plastic bag in a clean shop rag and handed it to me. "You hold that there for a little while, Benjamin. Gotta keep the swellin' down."

Jimmy went back to work while I sat in the office, holding ice to my finger. I could tell I hadn't broken it because I could wiggle it without a problem. I counted myself lucky for not having broken the skin. I looked around the office, windowless, illuminated only by a single lamp on the desk, and scanned the calendars and posters on the wall. Hal was an "aficionado of the female body"—those were his words—and I always marveled at how many pin-ups he had and how he changed them from time to time to update the decoration. He even had seasonal themes, like at Halloween, when he put up pictures of scantily clad "witches" straddling brooms or looking seductively at a scarecrow. The hormonal chaos going on inside my body was never helped by going into the office, where a kaleidoscope of long, nylon-encased legs, high heels gracing perfectly shaped feet and ankles, and lacy bra straps falling off shapely shoulders greeted me. The pictures inevitably made me wonder what Natalie would look like in those outfits. On that day, the pictures looked ridiculous.

I was determined not to stay too long because I wasn't in the mood for Hal's ribbing about doing anatomy studies in the office. Nor was I ready for the look my father would give me once he saw I'd nearly flattened my finger. I knew his look would just confirm, for him and me, my ineptness in the real world, a man's world. So I walked back to the wash bay where a white ghostly haze now cloaked the Olds' exterior. Jimmy was waiting for the wax to set, and as he stood back, I could see some of the gaps I left in my application. Jimmy filled these in as the haze became more pronounced. Then he noticed me.

"How's the thumb?" he said, smiling.

"Okay, more or less. It's lucky you got the ice so fast. It could've been a lot worse. Thanks."

Jimmy nodded. "Well, take a rag if you can, an' we can finish this baby."

I took one of the newly laundered blue cotton rags Jimmy had stacked in the wash-bay's cupboard and stood, waiting for his go-ahead. When everything was dry, Jimmy started and I followed. We polished and polished, but as before, my strokes were choppy while Jimmy's floated on free-jazz riffs. Swirling his rag, Jimmy's eyes had a translucent, far-off look. He was John Coltrane playing "Chasin' the Trane." Several times, saying nothing, he pointed to small waxy splotches I'd missed around one of the headlights or underneath the wiper blades. We sweated like we were in hell.

Almost like coming out of a trance, we stepped back to look at the gleaming Olds. We'd gone through at least a dozen rags, which now lay in a wax-encrusted heap on the floor. But Jimmy wasn't finished. Just when I thought the shine couldn't shine any more, Jimmy clutched a bottle of detailing spray, flared it back and forth, misting, swirled the cloth, stepped back, approached the car, sprayed and wiped again, then threw his rag into the bin at the back of the bay with a little flourish, like putting extra mustard on a slam dunk. Then I knew he was done.

Jimmy went into the back office to change his sweat-soaked shirt. I looked down at my thumbnail to see a garish sunset of purple, red, and deep bluish-black. In the next weeks I saw the colors crawl, glacier-like, from my lunula, the little white crescent at the base of the nail, to the tip of my pink nail plate. It was like watching a life grope along a broad plane of keratin and then disappear off the edge. I tried to use the nasty-looking nail to get Natalie's sympathy, saying I'd had "an industrial accident." Natalie just laughed; she wasn't going to be taken in by my sob story. We were finished, and she started dating a snarky guy who drove a fancy Chevelle Malibu SS-396. No way I could match that.

Several times Jimmy asked how the finger was and I said "fine." The swelling lessened after a few days, and I didn't take any time off work. Neither Hal nor my dad knew of the stupid accident, and there was no reason to tell them. They didn't even notice the multicolored nail; I made sure of that.

As August faded to September, there was a real industrial accident out on Fair Avenue where it crossed Empire. The green Dynamic 88 we'd worked on T-boned a burgundy Chevy Nova on a night hotter than the day. The Oldsmobile's driver, who'd given Jimmy a five-dollar tip for the wax job, which Jimmy then split with me, sustained only a few cuts and scratches. Not the driver of the Nova. At Jimmy's funeral, my mother and father, Hal, and I were the only white faces.

Later that day we were at the Smiths' home, crowded with relatives and friends and tables laden with food. I found myself standing before Jimmy's mother to give her my condolences. I shook her hand and said a single word: "James." Her response paralyzed me. I had expected a brave smile, a slight nod of recognition. Wasn't calling James by his proper name a small though significant step, a sign of respect? Instead I saw a tight-lipped bitterness. Her brown eyes glared in accusation. I felt like I'd thrown a stone into a deep well but couldn't hear—would never hear—the water splash. I wanted to say something more, but I knew my words were as useless as roadside litter.

Then it was time for the next mourner to pay respects, and I turned to walk out the front door. I didn't know where my parents were and I didn't care. I avoided the gaze of several customers I recognized from the station. After being in the crowded house, I thirsted for cool evening air, but the night was stifling. I walked for a block or two and felt a great distance open inside me.

Dying, Four Ways

Patricia Colleen Murphy

Maryland

Take your boat down to the Severn, drop
your crab pots. Ignore the cough and keep
smoking. Let the Cocker Spaniel pee on the
carpet. Try chemo and radiation, drink protein
shakes and Ensure. Have a lung out. Flatline in the
operating room, but fight your way back
so you can have 10 more months, during which
you will drive your Jeep up the street to Aloupis's
for Budweisers. Watch one more Orioles game.

Arizona

Lose your husband of 50 years while you
go blind. Leave the Bay for the Desert.
Complain about Bush/Cheney and eat
sandwiches while watching CNN. Flirt with
the paramedics. Tell everyone you have quit,
then sneak smokes all day. Buy identical
Tencel suits in 3 colors that you will never wear

because we're not going to go to Charleston's
for ribs anymore. Olive Garden, Hospitaliano.

Nevada

Wake up and make a pot of coffee. Take a
No-Doz or 3. Read an article from Harper's
while chewing Nicorette. Adjust your
cannula and turn off NPR. Walk back toward
your home office to start work for the day.
Clutch your chest, trip over the laundry
basket, and land face-down so that the blood
pools into your face like a bruise so bad
the coroner recommends a closed casket.

Ohio

Answer every phone call without fail. Lie
and say you went to the grocery store for
beans and metts. Lose 100 pounds. Let a
tumor grow so large you're blind in one eye.
Pretend you have a bad cold. At the hospital, ask to
be patched up and sent home. Give those who love
you five days to say goodbye. When I say,
"This is Jill. She has come to write the Will."
You say, "My name is Ed and I can be misled."

Night Sounds

Carmen K. Welsh, Jr.

Late evening and there was an all-night diner bearing the words *All-Nite*. The neon lights of the diner's name were dark in parts, as if someone had taken a bite from each letter. From the outside, the diner resembled a train car. That's what Mr. Castellano said I should expect, as well as the chrome-outfitted exterior, which had become dented and dingy with wear of the elements.

There was a walk-up and I opened the door. I balked when I entered the dimly lit diner. See, it had been just a few weeks since I had bussed in from Tennessee and Mr. Castellano wanted me to work for him. I wasn't used to a dog of his breed wanting to dine with a dog of my breed.

Once inside, I could see the space was narrow with a bar, and barstools. Patrons could face the interior window, where all sounds and smells wafted from the kitchen. Dogs were crammed in the homey yet narrow quarters. There was a single row of tables along the windows, giving it the feel of a train's diner car, and two tables were crammed in the rear, just by the back door. As I took a seat at a small empty table toward the front, I fitfully glanced about. Is it supposed to look like an omnibus? I thought. I had never seen anything like it. A ceiling fan lazily twirled.

There was a single waitress. She was long-haired and there were no signs of her ears, though she had pink barrettes to keep her hair out of her eyes, and markings that resembled grease stains. However, her waitress uniform was starched with only slight stains; her short, cuffed sleeves were no match for her furry arms.

"You want a glass of milk, dear?" the waitress asked two female customers. One of those customers was a tall woman with leathery, floppy ears under her skullcap, and her companion, a shorter woman with button ears and faded spots. "And your friend? Hey, Lew! One baby juice— no, make that two baby juices and a baled hay!" For the next fifteen minutes, I was probably the only customer watching the clock and my wristwatch instead of ordering any food. The waitress fired off implausibility after implausibility: one tube steak, seven Adam's ales, four deadeyes, one bossy in a bowl, as well as the most ridiculous phrase that made the other customers chuckle: "Burn one, take it through the garden, and pin a rose on it!" A table of male dachshunds clapped and hooted and the waitress winked at them before taking a bow.

"Order whatever before I get there," Mr. Castellano had told me. He'd winked and I felt particularly nervous by how casual and friendly his manner was. The diner's cacophony of smells and odors assailed my nose. The clock had a smiling face behind its two hands. It almost resembled the Mickey Mouse clocks I had seen in several shop windows since my arrival in the city. Surrounding the clock were news clippings, postcards, and pictures clipped from old ads and posters plastering the diner's walls.

I kept my tail away from the chair's slats so as not to disturb the gentleman behind me. The tables and chairs were too close and I didn't want to chance any altercation. My kind and type weren't wanted in most public places. I dared not lick my nose to make it more sensitive, an ingrained habit hounds have that help us sniff better. I felt uneasy because I was raised not to make it a habit of eating in strange places—only at church picnics and family gatherings.

Since I decided to take the table near the front, I could hear the incessant buzzing from the exposed diner lights. I wondered if the other patrons might have a problem with me being here. Two women sat with their backs to me, coats draped over the backs of their chairs. One woman's feathery tail wagged delicately so as not to disturb the tiny space the waitress and other customers had to pass through. Conversations were low and even the clinking of dishes was subdued. Only the waitress's grating voice broke through this muted atmosphere. Finally, she approached me.

"You want coffee, hon?"

"I'm waiting for someone."

"You can eat while waiting. What'll it be?"

"I'll just have coffee, thank you."

"No problem." The pot she held, she expertly tipped into one of the cups on my table and then scooted it toward me.

I didn't think long enough on how I got into this situation. I knew I was starving. No, not starving, just painfully hungry. Like my stomach had pinches in it. I decided to come before him, so in case I turned chicken, I could leave without a note. But that was being a coward, and my mama didn't bring me up that way. She also didn't bring me up to be waiting on strange men, or rather, awaiting a strange man.

I wanted to distract myself and took glances around the diner. The other folks had short fur or long fur. Their ears were poised or relaxed. I recognized a few dachshunds and setters. The other dogs were breeds I didn't readily recognize or were mixbred like me. I wondered if anyone was as hungry. Everyone here was like me, just regular dogs having a bite before heading home.

I wished I had taken that job my cousin wanted me to. I was far from home; in fact, I was in New York for the first time in my life. Though finding work grew harder and harder here, I still tried to look my best, in my nylons that hadn't run yet, my black shoes with straps. On my forepaws were gloves I tried to keep as white as I possibly could and on my head was a skullcap hat very much in style. It was the middle of summer, and I felt as angry as hungered. Why had I run away from home? If I was still there, I wouldn't have wanted for food. There were relatives I could stop by to see and they would automatically have a meal ready. There would always be a bite ready in case visitors dropped by or a loved one came with an unexpected guest. But waiting for someone in a diner that wasn't segregated spooked me. I couldn't get used to meeting here when it clearly meant that I was the only Basenji-mix around. I tried to see through the windows, but grease and other stains made the thick glass blurry. All I could hear were siren sounds and the occasional flash of a police cruiser.

Hadn't Mr. Castellano told me to order? I thought.

It didn't matter, because I was just as nervous as I was hungry. I hadn't eaten much, but I also would be meeting the dog that helped me in my first days in the city. And speak of the devil! The front door's bell jangled as Mr. Castellano stepped in. I hadn't known him very long but once he came in, I thought about a book.

What story was it? Oh Lord, the one Papa brought home on one of his brief visits. I thought of the first sentence in *Lord Jim* by Joseph Conrad: "He was an inch, perhaps two, under six feet, powerfully built, and he advanced straight at you with a slight stoop of the shoulders, head forward, and a fixed from-under stare which made you think of a charging bull."

And like the character from that book, Mr. Castellano came in hunched the same way. Though I didn't know exact inches, there wasn't a doubt he was well over six feet.

Even the other diners, who had not paid much mind when I came in, noticed him. He couldn't have snuck in if he tried. Mr. Castellano was in a medium-gray, double-breasted suit with pointed lapels. He kept his left paw in his trouser pocket. When he saw me, he grinned broadly and approached my table.

Why am I having supper with a total stranger and of such a strikingly different breed? I couldn't tell what dogs had made up Castellano. He resembled an all-white husky but had the build of a German shepherd. When he stood at my table, I felt I should get up. When he did sit down across from me, I greeted him.

"Comfy, Miss Hankin? Did you order anything? Want I should order for you?"

Castellano grinned again and I was grateful he didn't show much teeth. He had spotless white, well-groomed fur, pointed ears, and looked dashing in his suit. But he still rattled me a little. His wolf-like appearance did not help.

I couldn't kid myself; I found him attractive. When he turned his head and held up a paw to signal the waitress, his lupine profile was magnificent. His muzzle was angular and his snout almost pointed. His triangular ears would move forward as if he were always alert, and both ears had black tips as if someone had dipped them in ink. He had strong cheekbones and narrow eyes with longer lashes than I've seen on most male dogs. He had all-white, plush-looking fur. He could have been on a magazine cover.

Instead of continuing to gaze at him, I concentrated on my hunger and wondered what I should eat. The diner had all kinds of exciting new smells, both pleasant and not, but the most tantalizing was Mr. Castellano's. He had his own odor as well as cologne that smelled expensive. It seemed he had been designed by some fashion company. His suit's creases were razor-sharp. I wondered what he did for a living. Where did he get his money to dress so fine? Why did he dress this way but frequent eateries that catered to the working class? And then just as suddenly, I felt embarrassed.

"Yes. No, I didn't order yet. Thank you. You can call me Stacey. Is it supposed to look like an omnibus?"

"Yep, for the ambiance. And don't say that out loud. Or look around like that. Makes you seem like a tourist!"

"Sorry." I hung my head, trying to understand some of the odors. I thought I caught different soups and pork and gravy and butter sizzling, but I needed to pay attention to my host.

After all, he had invited me and I had accepted. Jobs were hard to come by, and I had run into some trouble at the employment lines. How would it look if my mind wandered? The clink of the dishes at different tables, the smells and sounds of bacon sizzling in the kitchen, made me salivate.

"You're uneasy, but don't worry. The longer you're here, the more joints I'll introduce you to."

Mr. Castellano seemed to have taken a shine to me. He had helped me out of what would have become a bad situation, had given me his business card, answered my call, and was now treating me to dinner. And I hadn't been in New York City for more than three and a half weeks! I could feel the pinch in my gut. I wanted to eat but my nervousness seemed to snap at me more. Such an invitation frightened me.

"Aren't you nervous? To be seen with me?" I asked.

"Should I? You've got rabies. Just say the word and I'll make like a banana and split!"

"No, I mean—" I glanced around. "Back home, I couldn't just come to any public place with you—especially a diner! They would refuse to serve me," I said.

Castellano took out a cigarette, put it in his mouth.

"If I thought you disliked me—" he began. I protested but he cut me off, continuing, "You mean how they separate dogs from dogs? Well." He took out a shiny pocket lighter. He held up two fingers in the air and signaled again to the waitress, who came to our table.

"And why didn't you order something, young lady?" She played stern with me. "You could've been eating while waiting for this mug!"

I lowered my gaze and felt my cheeks burn. Mr. Castellano chuckled.

"What you got for us tonight, Hortense?" he asked.

"For you, the blue plate."

"Tell your old man I don't want him cooking his socks again when preparing my steak."

Hortense laughed, "You're a killer as always, Slasher! Your usual, or you wanna mix it up tonight?"

"You know me—my usual." He did a Groucho impression by lifting his thick eyebrows rapidly. "But my friend here wants the best you've got, even if it ain't much!"

"Oh, that's okay! I can just have soup," I said.

"Ignore her. I'm paying! I'll trust you to pick something nice."

"Sure thing." Hortense turned to me, "Welcome to New York, hon!"

By the time I timidly said "thank you," I realized Mr. Castellano was right—I looked like a newcomer. The waitress called out, "Lew! One bossy in a bowl! Chicks on a raft, on the hoof, and a pair of drawers! And remember to paint it red, Lew!"

That doesn't sound like anything edible, I thought.

A mastiff-type, with bullish features and a tongue permanently hung out the left side of his jaw, suddenly stuck his head out from the interior window. "That sound like Slasher! Izzat you, Slasher?"

"It's me, Lew!"

"And he brought himself a lady friend! Had the poor girl waiting for him, too!"

"Now wait a minute—" Mr. Castellano said.

I wanted to curl into my chair. It seemed the more I tried to be invisible, the more attention I drew. I couldn't see the cook, but I heard him shout, "What, again?"

"No, I'm just—" Before I could stand, Castellano took my arm and pressed it for me to sit back down.

"Oh, and a bit of lumber," Hortense grabbed some toothpicks and brought them to Castellano. "I know you got an oral fixation!"

"I told you, stop analyzing me through them psychology books!"

"It's what I do! You think I wanna be here in this greasy joint, serving mugs like you the rest of my life?"

"Before you become a head shrink, how about using your talents to decide what my new friend wants?"

The waitress retreated to the kitchen.

"She looks like a customer who would take a chance," I heard the cook say to Hortense.

"Naw, she's strictly pigs in a blanket, like a hockey puck, dough well done with cow to cover, two deadeyes, and a side of Murphy."

What sort of language was that? I thought. None of that sounds appetizing! I worried I wouldn't get a good meal tonight. My stomach growled lower than I could and I pushed my forearm into my abdomen, hoping nobody heard but knowing somebody did.

"What about dessert?" Lew shouted.

"I'll leave that to you, Lew!" She winked at me before putting her tray under her arm to take another customer's order.

Castellano ate his eggs on toast and beef stew. His side of rare beef was slathered in ketchup. He also had a white porcelain cup of black coffee to his left. Hortense left an ashtray and his earlier cigarette. "Slow night," he said.

I nodded. I was relieved to see that the waitress and cook's strange lingo meant for me a ham sandwich, well-done, buttered toast, two poached eggs, and potatoes. We ate for a few moments in silence. Every now and then, I wondered what I had gotten myself into. The cleaning jobs and odd work might not last. General stores and major department stores would never hire me, a Basenji mix. I had the features inherited from my mother's side—a dull chestnut and white fur with the floppy ears of my Foxhound-mix father. These businesses still remain closed to most of the breeds in my family, specifically breeds that hail from Africa or the West Indies. I watched as Mr. Castellano dug into his food, lifted his head to take a look around, and then ate some more. He behaved as if constantly on the go, a bit nervous but not twitchy.

"Listen, kid. I've been thinking, I know it's short notice. You just got here, but… I've got a proposition for you."

I thought, Folks sure do move fast here. Did he just propose to me? Or am I being stupid and he means a business proposal? I was grateful for my sandwich. Had it been soup, I would have spilled it, and how would that look to a sophisticated gentleman like Mr. Castellano? He must have seen my expression and felt my scent change in my awkwardness.

"No no no, kid! Sheesh! I don't work that fast!" Instead of being cross, he began to laugh, "Boy, you sure are something, Stacey Hankin!"

Of course not. I thought. Who am I kidding? I'm just some country hound dog he finds amusing.

Just three weeks before, I'd left the place of my birth to find better chances up north, against my mother's wishes. I had been sent back to her family's small, rural community, where a dog either sharecropped or farmed and little else. Yet, New York had been proving hard hit and folks of all kinds stood in lines for hours. Those not picked that day had to find a shelter to rest in until the next morning. The shelters were stretched to capacity, and having some unrecognized hound from the south appeared just the type of excuse these city dogs needed to start an altercation.

They had tried to intimidate me from the line, especially since I was one of the few females in line. I hadn't wanted to argue, but I was jostled and pushed away. The agency folks did little to stop the dispute; they were exhausted city workers with their own troubles.

I had insisted on stepping back into my place in line and that's when the situation took a turn. I was forcibly removed, even pushed by my shoulder, and the aggressor shouted bigoted words into my face. When I stepped back in once more, I was attacked, my face slapped. My only thought was: I'm about to be killed. I just left home to come up north and now I'm going to be killed. Only my family would have missed me, and they knew by then I was missing. I felt sick to my stomach.

It was either remembered guilt or I had eaten my meal too quickly.

Mr. Castellano had come from nowhere; he punched and elbowed my attackers. Some dropped flat like a bag of bricks hit them. The crowd dispersed. The city workers immediately put up signs that the lines were closed. There would be no more openings that day. Mr. Castellano and I became acquainted after that incident.

"I hear you're beatin' the pavement." Mr. Castellano's statement brought me out of my reverie.

"But I've got a job, Mr.—"

"Slash, Slasher, any of those, but please, not Mr. Castellano! You sound like my tailor! Which is why I'm bringing this up!" His tone changed quickly: "How would you like to work for me?"

"Doing what?" My imagination reeled and I felt horribly embarrassed. What was wrong with me? I could only credit my behavior to how nervous and confused I became when around him.

I have no idea what you do for a living! I thought. You wear expensive clothes, you smell expensive, and "You could be running a hootchie-kootchie show for all I know, oh Lord…"

I lowered my face and covered my eyes when I realized I had said that out loud.

Castellano burst out in laughter, and it was hearty and confident. It's a good thing he was a regular patron; if this were anywhere else, we might have been thrown out.

"I like you, Hankin! I see we're gonna get along real swell! But back to my proposal. You ain't half-bad, so don't sell yourself short! With the way you dress and carry yourself, you may just be what I'm looking for!" He moved his empty plates to the side and clasped both paws, setting them on the table before he leaned toward me.

"You're a Southerner, so you might know some things. Got any experience in…distilling?"

"You mean…" I lowered my voice, "…moonshine?"

Castellano grinned, "Sure. Booze. But we do it kind of different here. I've got a good size operation. Could be bigger, but I'm workin' on that. You interested?"

I thought everyone could hear my heart pounding "But isn't that—?

"Listen, I know you're a straight-shooter, from the looks of you. But I'm sure you've taken a look around."

He had watched me watching everything. Since coming to New York, I had never seen so many different dogs! And in this finite space, this diner showed part of the city in one room.

In the diner's corner, close to the kitchen entrance, a brown, curly-haired dog sat alone.

"You mean like the curly gentleman over there?" I noticed him as one of the nondescript dogs whose breed I couldn't figure out. He was a sad and sorry sight. He wore a suit a size blessedly larger. His shoes may have been scuffed, but since the diner was so narrow and the tables so close together, it would be hard to see what shoes the other patrons wore. Mr. Castellano's tall frame was already too much for the narrow table where we both sat.

"Is he like a…sheepdog, or…?" I was learning. Perhaps there were too many that were unfamiliar to me.

"That guy's a poodle," Mr. Castellano said. "He's a regular. He comes here every night and nurses the same bowl of tasteless broth. He barely has the pennies to scrape together for a potato. See? He seasons it with the pepper and salt shakers. He can't even afford potatoes in that soup!"

"Poor man." I noticed now he must have gotten his suit from a mission house. My mother and aunts had worked and run enough clothing drives in our community that I could tell the origin of the man's poor-fitted suit.

"You're used to seeing poodle models in those catalogs and magazines. But grooming and heavy trimming, like what most poodles require, costs dough! Tomorrow, that poor schlub will be back in the line again, trying to get something, anything. But he won't. And he'll be in another flophouse, if he can make it in time for the curfew. If not, another night on the streets. It's not like the old days, honey. Being a stray was tough, but never like this."

"What will happen to him?"

"Like many others, he'll get in a fight, or someone will try to roll him. He's too old. He won't last much longer."

I felt my throat constricting. I quickly tapped the tears from my lashes.

"Sorry, kid. Didn't mean to upset you. That's why I want you to work for me. It's hard here. Harder even for certain dogs. Now, that poodle may just get something, anything, if he can just get the two bits to get himself spit and shined. But you, what will you be doing?"

"I guess…maybe housekeeping. I might even be able to find some more cleaning jobs."

"Is that what you wanna be doing?"

"It's work. It's… I'm not judging you, Mr. Castellano, but it's…" I squirmed then because I wanted to say "honest." I didn't.

"Yeah. But where will it get you?"

I stared out the window. There were old newspapers stuck under the crevices of the diner.

Mr. Castellano went to drinking his second cup of coffee. While he sipped—and he even did that with elegance—I tried to shake off my frustration. In the window's reflection, I could hear police cruiser sirens nearby. Folks shouted further away. I noticed that Castellano heard those night sounds as well. His pointed left ear twitched every now and again. I cocked my own ear toward the window, picking up more noises. I was staying in a boardinghouse and didn't want to be late for curfew. I slipped my finger under my watch's wristband to adjust it.

Stars

Eva Skrande

I am the daughter of everything old.
With each breath, like a gray boat
I am closer to my final home.

I am the daughter of five old fingers
sewing the eternal quilt.
I am the eldest daughter

of the moon, her wheat.
My dress of light tearing among the branches.
With each old step I take

I rise higher.
I am the old daughter of old stars
that live off of my rising breath.

"Untitled (After Nomura)" by George Davis Cathcart

THE VELVET HOUR

MK AHN

She is in Hae-un-dae, the resort town by the dark blue sea. Where the Busan Film Festival spills onto the autumn beach and into the salty air.

Here in Hae-un-dae, the day is ripe. Lemon-yellow light trickling into last night's darkness, brightening the silence in the hotel room. She opens her eyes. He is no longer lying beside her. She sees only small patches of wetness absorbed into the white pillowcase.

She is here for the film premiere. She is here as an imposter. She is taking a break from her screenplay to write a review of the film he is in, Director Hong's *The Turning Gate*. (It's her only way into the sold-out screening.) Although it already has positive buzz, she doubts it can live up to Director Hong's first film, *The Day a Pig Fell into a Well*.

Today, the air is light, still warm for September, but not as moist. She looks out the window at the children playing on the beach, oblivious of his film, oblivious of his hair. "*Bbali su-young-*

haja!" they scream. "Let's swim! Let's jump into the sea!" She stares at the rows and rows of parasols over families of tanned bodies, and thinks of her brother. He must be wondering where she is. And if she's looking for Unni, the Elder Sister. Instead, she's looking for the actor, wanting to run her fingers through his hair, smell his signature scent of soap, the generic flowery sweet kind. She wants to glide her tongue up the back of his neck, taste the skin rich with last night's sleep, his pores exhaling alcohol from his body. But he is no longer beside her. She knows she should not go after him; he is not for her. But somehow this makes her want him even more.

She finds him later that night at the Wide Angle party. But first she sees Cate. Cate watching him fall off his chair onto the floor of the crowded bar. Cate trying not to laugh. The same Cate who had introduced them a month earlier; who'd slept with him before, who decided he was just a fling, who said, "He likes pretty girls. And you need to get laid!" The same Cate who was also searching for family here in Korea. The same Cate who wrote a song for his film.

She watches from the perimeter of the long, narrow bar as he gets back on to the chair. Cate sits next to him, whispering in his ear. But he turns away from Cate, and sees her, calling her over with the flick of a hand; though they have known each other for a month, it is the first time she's seen him impatient with her. And it makes her happy.

"You're such a pretty girl," he says to her. "Will you be responsible for me tonight?"

"Yes," she says with her eyes, though she wants to keep watching him choose her.

"You're strange," he says. He doesn't want her in the perimeter any longer.

There are other things he thinks strange: Long nails with short hair. Long nails with low voice. To him, she's more boy than girl.

She thinks these contradictions suit her well, these paradoxes of length and tone. Category and consistency have never worked for her. She is neither nor—or—left in between. She wonders if it was the same for the mother she never knew, if this is why her mother disappeared years ago.

At the end of the evening, the music at the party deteriorates into some kind of hard-rock thrash that distorts the speakers. He is so drunk, he wants to dance anyway. He lifts his arms to the side, letting all that scotch and beer guide him, moving to the monotonous music she can no longer hear. His smile says he is barely there.

She sees Cate on the other side of the dance floor, and walks to her.

"Do you think he's okay?" She feels Cate moving away.

"Shhhhh," Cate says with her finger, looking at him.

What is Cate afraid of? She doesn't care what he thinks.

"I'm worried about him," she says into Cate's ear. "I think he might spiral."

"I can't imagine the spiral," Cate says. "He's not like that."

"Did you ever see him depressed?" she asks.

Cate looks past her at the others dancing. "Why are you taking him so seriously? Can't you just have fun?"

When he walks toward them, Cate walks off.

She doesn't see Cate again that night. Cate didn't say goodbye; she usually says goodbye.

Despite the spots he says are growing on his liver, he insists on drinking more. He tosses the herbal regenerative pills she gives him back with beer. He's made a pact with Director Hong to get drunk every day for a year. He says he has nothing better to do, because it gives him purpose.

Every night he drives himself into himself, giving in to Crown Royal and Cass. Just like the others she sees running from themselves only to end up someplace they have already been: Cate running away from her ex-husband in Minneapolis. Aunt Komo running away from Korea, from family, into more loneliness in Chicago. Just like them, she's been running most of her life, too, toward things she cannot name, things she can probably never find. She thought she was running in the right direction this time, toward a sister who might be able to explain why.

But then she found him.

They dance slowly through another couple songs at the party, ignoring the thrashing beats. The cobblestone alley comes next. Then the shuffling into midnight. She notices a flicker of recognition in the shop owners closing up, as if they want to yell, "Sign, Mr. Park, sign!" But they leave them to stumble through the twilight.

She likes how the darkness feels on her skin, smooth and soft like velvet. She pulls him by the shoulder of his suit. All six feet of him. The shuffling gets louder and louder, and then she sees grey. Somehow he finds the rest of the way home.

The colors begin to fade at the hotel front desk. He is getting a second room.

"People will talk," he says.

"I don't care what they think," she says.

"We can't be seen going into my room," he insists. "They will photograph us."

He falls off his chair, yet he arranges these details.

On the bed she wants to cry. She can feel a sadness deepening between them, his aimlessness pulling him away. She turns her head to let go of the tears. Then she hears a slap-slap against the ceiling. Her eyes focus, and there he is, naked, his penis flaccid, a newspaper rolled in his hand as he hunts the mosquito.

She fades some more on her knees. Then he is behind her, rocking himself inside her. His aimlessness now directed at her. She sees black as wetness spills from her eyes. He blurs beside her, and she knows she might disappear.

She thought the impending premiere would make him happier, but it doesn't matter enough. She can see him fighting himself, through his silence and monotone, fighting to uncover what he really wants. Maybe he is like her—grasping for something that will render everything else meaningless; that can lead him into his own desire. He just hasn't found it yet. And she hasn't found it yet either. But something keeps her in that aimless room. Just like some days she can't get off the train at her designated stop. She knows she should get up. She knows she will be late. Yet nothing can get her to go. She doesn't know what it is except she can't pull herself out of the aimlessness. Not yet.

He is standing again with the newspaper. The mosquitoes give him purpose; he knows the buzzing overhead can turn dangerous. They have already suffered multiple bites. Three bites on her left leg, one on the forehead, and two on the neck, all the size of egg yolks. Swollen noses, drained of blood, turned a rare-steak kind of red. He told her to douse them in calamine lotion but it smells too medicinal.

"They can't keep taking my blood," he says with a strange quiver. "I won't let them."

He usually doesn't make a sound when he sleeps, curled up into himself, breathing lightly. But that night in his dreams, he makes a song in her ears, a soft, tender gasping for breath.

They wake the next morning unscathed. He must have gotten the bloodsucker, splattered it all over the ceiling. Or maybe it was the dragons he spoke of in his dreams, floating up and lashing the ceiling with their lizard-length tongues.

He sits up in bed and lights a cigarette. "Why did you cry last night?"

"Because," he answers when she doesn't, "you cry because."

She cried because he was beautiful that first night in Seoul at the *soju* bar. His floppy chestnut-brown hair—the way it fell into his eyes, the way he pushed it from his face—brought both desire and sadness, made her feel she'd lost something she never had. (Why does he keep pulling his hair from his face, when it always falls back?)

She cried because they made an abstract painting with blood that night.

"Beautiful," he'd said, pointing at the sheets. "A Rorschach test, or perhaps a Pollock."

She was surprised he wanted to look. She wanted to hide the evidence.

The other men she'd been with were terrified of the monthly remnants, these spots of scarlet. "A crime scene," one had said.

But his voice was smooth, calm as he continued to admire the sheets. As if he were losing himself in the patterns of blood.

She cried because of his symmetry. Each feature so balanced, distinct. It made her think she only wanted him. She hadn't been able to write anything for weeks. She needed something to shape the watery days, to engulf, to overwhelm; something that could save her from the silence of the blank page.

She cried because of his question: "What do you think of me?"

To which she replied (variously):

"I think you're self-destructive."

"I think you don't know who you are."

"You're brilliant in your self-destructiveness, tragic in your ignorance."

"You can't translate yourself."

"I think you won't stop."

He said: "I think you're right; I find myself like this. Always on the phone with a girl, talking late at night. What if I told you I wanted to kill myself? What would you do?"

She said, "Is it wrong if that's what you want?"

"You're right," he said with eerie acceptance. "I want what I want."

He allowed her in with his recklessness.

She cried because even as he engulfed her, she knew she could never have him—he was not something to keep or hold onto. That's what drew her to him in the first place. She was attracted to the idea of impermanence; it was useless for her to hang on to things that couldn't be held.

But that didn't stop her. It never did.

After he finishes his last cigarette in the hotel room, they make love one more time before he leaves for an interview. He waits for her orgasm. He wants her to tell him when that release comes—sitting on top of him—because he needs to know. He's fascinated at how her body can disintegrate into climax, how it lives so deep inside. She likes how he can soften the sharpness. She knows she shouldn't, but she can't imagine not having the possibility.

"What does it feel like?" he asks. "The orgasm. I can't feel so much in mine."

"Like everything is finally okay," she says.

She doesn't love him, but holds on to him with her own recklessness.

The song he made in her dreams lingers in the hotel room as she tries to take out her contact lenses. Only stars and strands of blood come out from her eyes, blood branching through the whites. She rubs and scrapes until they are bright red, realizing later, through the dizzy shape of the late afternoon, that she'd already taken the lenses out, and put them in a glass of water. But it is too late. The room has already been cleaned, the water dumped, the lenses lost.

So she watches the films through the branches of blood.

The air is thick, guiding her from film to film. Most others retreating into the theaters. As she watches the third film in a row, a German feature with no dialogue, her head begins to numb.

But then everything by the dark blue sea shifts to Cate. He confesses about it on the main plaza, among the masses of people queued in front of the box office. Cate will be by his side that evening for the film premiere. Her Cate. Their Cate. The Cate who made them more stylish. The Cate who'd brought them together. Once he sees the media encroaching, he guides them slowly in and out of the crowds into the alleyway between the two theaters. It is rumored that Maggie Cheung has arrived for the premiere of 2046.

She admires his honesty, his calm, as if it is perfectly logical that he should be Cate's for the second evening, the evening of the premiere. His manager has just decided on Cate, the musician, the media darling, the one who can boost his image. She hates that Cate will be responsible for him that night, but she smiles, says okay. She thinks about her brother again back in Seoul, how he ignored the actor that accidental night of singing and drinking; how he could never know she was here with him. A sharpness shoots through her brow, and she swallows hard. She's been ignoring her brother's calls. But the image of his hands, his lips, make the back of her head swell a bit more; so she wanders the crowded streets, the air still heavy on her skin, until she finds the ice cream cart. She eats soft serve until she can no longer feel her head.

She arrives at the film premiere late, alone, the sold-out crowd silently engrossed. The actor plays a married professor who pays for a bar hostess who doesn't want him to touch her hair. Instead, she wants him to hurry. "*Bbali!*" she shrieks from the bed. "Hurry up and finish!"

Director Hong found him, raw, his talent hidden. He refused the director's requests to cut his hair and fix his gold fillings, and though he didn't mind acting, those sex scenes weren't easy.

She watches him walk onto the stage afterward, modest and shy. He waits for questions from the giggly teenage girls. He answers a simple, "No" and they scream in ecstasy. When he walks away, they scream again, "Sign, Mr. Park, sign!"

She is wrong. Director Hong is no one-hit wonder. And she is right. The actor is a star now. Director Hong has praised him as one of the best non-actor actors.

The actor sees her on the outer perimeter of the screaming girls. She pushes closer to him and says she will see him later. Her deadline for the *Korea Times* is looming. She needs to see another film.

She leaves the screening early, and finds him standing outside the theatre. He is blowing cigarette smoke onto all the mosquitoes in the plaza, the plaza that is electric with his film.

Sign, Mr. Park, sign!

He looks elegant in that perfect suit. She waits for him to sign one more autograph, but Cate reaches him before she can whisper how perfect he is. (She wants to see his gold smile.)

"*Mosshisseo!*" Cate says to him in the steamy air of the plaza. "*You're beautiful!*"

Then the photographers circle him.

Later, he calls her from the cab, his voice jittery as the taxi speeds toward the beach. She can almost see him leaning into Cate with the sharp turns of the cab. She is back in her room, resting her stomach. She expected a separation, but he lures her in again with his honesty, his 'everything will be okay.'

So she meets him on the beach, by his favorite seafood cart. The dusk air is wet, the sky lavender, brooding. Cate is there beside him wearing a suit—the two of them in their tailored suits—almost as if it was planned all along. But next to his, Cate's is almost as unremarkable as the wide-eyed girls from before.

Cate says, "I want to jump into the sea!"

She no longer knows Cate.

"You should jump in too!" Cate continues.

But the *ajumahs* say a typhoon is coming.

"I'm an American!" Cate yells as she bats away the mosquitoes.

What does she have to prove?

"And you are, too!" Cate pulls her closer to the water.

She doesn't have anything to prove.

"We are Koreans, too, in Korea!" Cate runs around in circles. "We can do anything here!"

She looks around and can't see him. He is probably already eating the fist-shaped cartilaginous sea creatures. The ones that self-combust into orange flames on the mobile food carts. Why is she on that beach with Cate trying to pull her into the ocean?

She wonders if he will sleep with Cate that night.

But she cannot ask.

I'm an American!

Cate's bland face could never match his beauty.

I could stay on this beach forever!

The sand is velvet on her bare feet, but she is beginning to hate the sound of Cate. She doesn't want to be American anymore.

Luckily, the jellyfish they enjoy on the beach is enough of a distraction. The dull slippery crunch of them feels so good in her mouth, she almost doesn't care about the rest of the evening. The sea has turned restless, the smell now salty from slightly sour. The rows of food carts continue searing and grilling, chopping and frying, with only the *ajumahs* pacing up and down, policing the beach and the reckless Americans.

"Look at how well-preserved he is," Cate says, looking at him. They are all sitting at the food cart. "Do you know how old he is?"

She has never heard Cate speak this way; but he acts as if he's heard it all before, turning his head away from Cate.

"He's so visual," Cate continues. He rolls up his sleeves to assess the bites on his arm. "See how worried he is?"

"You can't do anything about it," Cate tells him. "They're going to keep taking your blood."

She looks down at Cate's exposed legs beneath the cart. Enormous bites on her shin, knee, and calf. Cate slaps at her legs the most, but they still look sepulchral. The bites will swell into even larger pink mussel rounds. He is slapping and scratching as well, even though he is covered up in his suit. These mosquitoes are three times the size of any stateside, stealthy too, hovering, sniffing blood. How much can they suck from one person?

"Has he spiraled yet?" Cate asks while he goes to the washroom.

"Just drinking a lot," she says.

"Don't worry," Cate says. "He'll be okay."

She doesn't want to know what Cate knows of his binges.

She wants to remind Cate that they are the result of her and all her questions:

Do you like him?

I don't want his number.

Why won't you meet him?

He's too beautiful.

You're both in the film biz.

It would never work.

Besides, you have to get laid!

He's your ex.

I'm totally over him. It was just a fling.

She knows she should have stopped herself but she couldn't.

Are you really over him? she wants to ask Cate.

But Cate is running around in circles again. She feels pieces of herself breaking apart.

Do I need to get laid?

A pain expands in her center.

Whose fling is it?

A dull but persistent kind of ache. She wants to care less.

She moves toward the tall waves as they fall onto the beach. He runs after her, and carries her back to the room.

"Will you take care of me?" he asks as he lays her on the bed.

"I have to take care of myself first," she says. And then passes out.

Today is the last day of the film festival. The light is still lemon-yellow; the blue dragons of his dreams still fly around in her head. The kids still laugh on the beach, though softer now. And he is still not beside her.

She sits up on the bed in the hotel room. Her body still aches. She opens the window and smells the salty air. She sees a man with floppy brown hair walking toward the sea, and thinks it is him. Of course, he's just gone out for a quick dip, a quick walk in the moist air. But then the man turns, and he is not him. He is younger; he is not beautiful.

Staring at the sea, she realizes she cannot love enough. Although his beauty still engulfs her, she cannot take care of him. She does not want him to completely disappear.

There is a knock on the door; she looks through the peephole and smiles. Cate has finally returned for him, but her eyes are unsettled; for a moment, she pictures him in the bathtub, the drip of metallic scarlet spidering into the water. Is this what he's decided? He was so worried about the mosquitoes taking his blood; and now he's taking his own?

She walks into the bathroom and he's not there. She turns away from the door, away from Cate, toward the lemon yellow and sparkling blue. She will not let Cate tell her about him. She will look out the window and see his hair all shiny and new. She will see the back of him shimmering in the deep blue sea; and she will wrap herself into the silence enclosing the room.

SALT LOVE

George Bishop

to a passenger

Like an empty ferry slip
late at night—that opening,

creosote feathering loose
lines in air older than love,

salt stinging in the shallows
of her stare anymore, that

stoic after-face of faith healed
of memory, dead at the edge

of herself. She's waited long
enough, then a little more.

She's the night of us all,
steady, on schedule, a heart

always a beat behind saving
what's sinking in her eyes.

"Untitled" by George Davis Cathcart

A MONTH OF SWALLOWS

LAUREN GENOVESI

The plan was to arrive in Medan separately, so if one of them got caught it wouldn't be back to tsunami camp for everybody. The whole thing was Theo's idea. His news-obsessed dad had mentioned the bird houses back in New York—these concrete block buildings constructed across Northern Sumatra to lure swiftlets—birds whose nests were one of the most expensive delicacies in the world. Swiftlets built nests from their saliva and attached them to the walls of the caves where they lived his dad said, bringing up a photograph of one on his laptop. Its half-circle shape was like a holy water receptacle made of ice.

Not that Theo was really paying attention to his father at the time. The nest only popped back into his head many weeks later when he was trying to figure out a way to stop Issa from sleeping with Derrick, one of the other tsunami volunteers. Having a conversation with her about being exclusive somehow seemed more of a risk than the drastic plan of escape that he proposed: Along with another couple, they would break out from volunteer camp, travel to Medan, and squat in one of the bird houses until they got caught or sick of it, whichever came first. Issa was miserable at volunteer camp—her parents had forced her to come—and he suspected she would go for it. She did.

Theo was the first to arrive. The building looked just like its Google Earth picture—three stories of stubborn concrete. The tsunami had barely disrupted it aside from some slight tilting, but even that could've been Theo's imagination. A chimney-like rectangle poked out from the tree-line of a dense forest not far from the beach.

He went inside and climbed both sets of steps. White splatters of bird shit and tufts of feathers decorated the floors, but no nests were built. It seemed unlikely that they were recently collected, considering the near-absurd stillness of this place. He had encountered exactly zero people on his walk after the city limits. It had been almost a month since the storm, but people were still afraid to come out of the crevices, like rats hiding underneath subway tracks. Not that Theo was complaining. They would be able to hide here, unbothered, for a month or two before anyone from the volunteer camp tracked them down and called their parents.

On the third floor, Theo dropped his bag to stake claim on the most private area of the house for himself and Issa. Three grey birds with alien heads hovered in the center of the room, crossing paths as if they were taking turns being each point on a triangle. He watched them for a while, but was interrupted by two voices. He went downstairs to greet them.

I thought we agreed to arrive separately, Theo said.

Jesse and Margot smiled at each other.

We didn't get caught, Jesse said.

That's not the point.

Don't be mad cause you and Issa didn't get to make out on the bus, said Jesse, grabbing Margot's waist with his grossly long fingers.

Stop, Margot mock-whispered, as if Theo couldn't hear.

Theo turned to leave the house.

Where are you going? Margot called after him. Do you know when Issa will be here?

Theo felt them laughing and kissing and probably fucking as he pushed through the woods to the beach. The crashing waves shushed him. He took off his shoes and gripped his toes in the sand, every forceful step fueled by his irritation at himself for inviting Jesse and Margot along on this trip. But Issa would have never agreed to come with Theo alone. And aside from Derrick, those were the two from camp she seemed to like best, although it was hard to tell with Issa. She was always laughing and joking with everyone—including Theo, it sometimes seemed—equally.

Theo was alone in the house when he got back. He walked up the two sets of stairs, laid out his sleeping bag, and slid his purple velvet satchel of condoms underneath the pillow. He regarded his bed for several minutes, then walked to the oval window. The sun wasn't yet down. Birds hopped from tree to tree. Soon, Theo heard Jesse and Margot come back inside. Issa was not with them. An hour passed, Theo sitting cross-legged on top of his sleeping bag listening to Jesse and Margot worry aloud about all of the horrible complications that could've delayed her journey. Finally, they decided to trek out to the Plan B meeting spot. They called up to Theo that they were going. He called back down to go without him. Several hours passed, and Jesse and Margot returned, again without Issa. Now, they were really worried—sure she had died or worse. Theo started to consider the possibilities, but he was somehow sure that Issa was safe. That the only person to whom something bad had happened was him.

He must have slept eventually, because Issa's voice woke him around eight. She called out from the bottom of the steps, the raspy familiarity sending fire across his belly. Margot squealed, and there were sounds of hugging, the dropping of Issa's bag. He dressed frantically and started down. At the top of the second staircase, where there was a bend, he saw her. Her face was flushed and balmy, her legs meaty and tanned against the frayed edge of her white cutoffs.

Where were you?

The anger was in his voice like smoke gets in a jacket. Margot dropped her eyes.

She was just telling us, Jesse said. So you missed the bus out of Medan. Did you sleep in the station?

No, I went back.

For Derrick, obviously. Issa ran toward the steps, brushing Theo's lips with a quick kiss on her way past him to look at the rest of the house. Of course for Derrick, but at least she seemed guilty.

It's pretty dirty, Theo said to her back. But I made a space for us. On the top floor.

He followed her up and put his arms around her. When she turned and kissed him back, his body flooded and sloshed with heat. Tenderness. He had been wrong about everything. Derrick had never existed. But then Theo opened his eyes, and meeting her gaze was like walking into the same glass door he had not seen a dozen times before. Still. Still. She was not letting him through.

Back downstairs, everyone prepared to go to the beach. They would have to be out of the bird-house all day every day, in case any nest-messengers came to collect. And in case the messengers did come, no clues of the squatters' presence could visible. Theo led the clean-up commission, to be repeated every morning. Each person packed his or her belongings and stowed them in the closet on the roof. Then they each combed a section of the house to make sure it was clear of nests. If the messengers found none, they would have less reason to return.

Theo was still inspecting when they called to hurry up. But they had all been in too much of a rush to get to the beach, and he wanted to do some quality-control. And sure enough, he found a large fragment that had been overlooked. It was in the section Issa had been assigned. A narrow sheath like a segment of a corn husk. When he peeled it from the wall, it left a film on his fingers at once chalky and greasy.

A little ways down the beach, Jesse and Margot each took two corners of their sheet, the wind punching it from underneath. Theo nodded his head at Issa to keep on.

What's wrong with this spot? Issa said.

I like it down a little further.

You're not gonna sit with us? Jesse said.

Theo had not stopped walking. Issa laughed and ran after him. She jumped on his back and stuck there, barely shaking him. He was her pillar, she would not miss Jesse and Margot at all. He imagined himself expanded to King Kong proportions, tearing through a city with Issa clinging to his back. Still carrying her, he spread out their sheet beneath them, then flipped her over his shoulder and unfolded her gently. She protected her eyes from the sun with her forearm and sprawled out. He used water from the bottle they brought to clean his hands.

When it was time to get supplies, Theo insisted on walking the three miles to the central city market.

There's one five blocks that way, Jesse said.

I know there is. That's not the point.

Don't be so paranoid, Jesse said. People have better things to do than pay attention to four white idiots.

Theo kept walking.

I guarantee we're the only customers in that market anyway.

When Theo failed to answer again, Jesse huffed, but followed them.

The central market was acceptably large and populous, but Theo wanted to get in and out quickly. He raced up and down rows of chili peppers and sun-heated metal scales as the others dawdled and browsed. Issa and Margot linked pinkies and swung their arms, Jesse trailing behind. Theo met them on the way out—a hall tree dangling with plastic bags of produce and meat, including two bowling pin-shaped, red-stained pig legs.

Back at the house, on the floor atop their eating mat, Theo measured out portions of meat based on how long it would last without refrigeration. Margot shook her head, reminding Theo for the second or third time that she was a vegetarian. Good, more for them. Jesse ate and looked around the table for what else he could choke down. Issa shrugged at her plate. She was not a vegetarian. She was from Houston.

You don't want it? Jesse said.

It tastes like soap.

A swiftlet flew past, its large, proud eye fixed on the food, but then it flitted straight out the window. No one, besides Theo, even noticed.

That's right, he said to the bird.

You're crazy, Jesse said to Issa. I'll split it with you?

I'm good, said Theo.

They were drunk by the time they went to bed, but Theo suspected that Issa was exaggerating her inebriation—all flopping limbs and repeated insistence that the room was spinning—to get out of sex. His feelings were hurt. But instead of trying to convince her, he turned toward the wall.

I caught Jesse snooping in your travel pouch today, he said.

My travel pouch? What is this you refer to as my travel pouch?

Just watch your money, is all I'm saying.

Not like there's not plenty to go around.

Soon there won't be. And as soon as somebody uses a credit card, we're caught.

Oh my God, Theo.

Oh my God, what?

Just don't try to make this last forever.

A few mornings later, when everyone else had left for the beach, Theo was on the roof shoulder-deep in Issa's pack. He felt the money pouch, brought it over the side of the bag, and scraped it up the side with a nylon sound. Then he heard two voices. He quickly zipped Issa's bag closed and restored it to its former position before remembering that stealing Issa's money was not the thing he would get in trouble for with the messengers.

He ducked down with the luggage and listened as they inspected the first two floors. He understood none of their clucking but felt he knew what they were expressing—surprise about the lack of nests. They each stepped onto the roof, but only barely. As they made their way down the stairs, Theo stayed in the closet with his cheeks burning for ten minutes before he dragged his own pack out and pushed Issa's money to the bottom. Then he went to the beach to meet the others, who teased that he was lying about the messengers to scare better morning inspections out of them. They were only kidding, but it made Theo wonder if he had imagined the footsteps, the clucking.

Days passed, and Issa mentioned nothing about the missing money. She must have noticed: Theo had taken more than half of what she had. This meant two things. First, she believed it was Jesse who stole from her, and second, she was willing to lie to Theo to protect him.

One morning at the beach about a week later, Theo put his sheet down next to Jesse's and Margot's instead of marching past them.

What's this? Margot said. You're getting sick of each other? What a coincidence.

She looked at Jesse, who rolled his eyes but took Margot's head in the crook of his elbow, kissed her hair. They separated and each settled onto the blanket in ways that made Theo think of people lowering themselves into coffins.

I could never be sick of Issa, Theo said, not looking at anyone.

Wearing his black T-shirt and jean shorts, he walked into the water. He was not swimming; he was bathing. When he emerged, he wrung out his shirt and hung it on a tree branch at the edge of the beach to dry. The money pouch dangling around his neck dried in the sun. With Issa and Jesse still in the water, he walked back to the blanket.

Margot lay on her stomach, a pool of sweat gathering at the back of one knee and not the other. Theo splashed the puddle and rubbed it into her thigh. She looked up from her book, puzzled.

Sorry, he said in monotone. I couldn't help myself.

The sarcasm chandeliered out from his voice, and Margot seemed confused by its contradiction with the affectionate gesture. He was not concerned about explaining. He stretched out his elbows and made a cup for his head with woven hands. Margot supposedly went back to reading, but as Theo pretended to sleep, he listened for a turning page and heard none.

That evening, Theo walked to the market by himself and came back with a sack of lychees, a bottle of rum, and a large glass jar with a lid. Jesse and Issa had gone out to smoke.

Lychees? said Margot. My favorite.

Issa's, too.

What do you mean? She just tried her first one at the market the other day. I peeled it for her.

I didn't know you needed a ton of practice to like something.

Why'd you get so many?

I could tell you but I'd have to kill you.

He wouldn't let anyone near him in the hours he spent preparing the fruit. Which he unveiled after dinner the next night, unsealing the jar and distributing the rum-soaked lychees.

Disembodied from their heavy seeds, the fleshy parts of the fruit hung in limp, amorphous shapes like animal hides. They dipped their heads back to swallow them whole.

What do you think? Theo asked Issa.

Delicious!

Really wonderful, Margot started to say, but Issa moved to Theo's lap and blocked Margot's eye contact. From Issa, this was the reaction Theo had been hoping for—adoration, the promise of sex, appreciation. But it was not hitting for him. He had to keep forcing his eyelids closed as she kissed him.

Do you want to go for a walk? he heard Margot ask Jesse from what felt like under water. Jesse said maybe in a while, then they were silent for several seconds, which Issa didn't seem to notice. She tried to move onto his neck, but Theo got embarrassed and shook her off.

Sorry! she said, turning around. What are we doing now?

To be honest, I'm ready to go to bed, Theo said. I just realized.

He got up to move toward the stairs, but Issa pulled him back down to the mat.

Wait! Issa said. I want to hang out some more.

Right? said Jesse. That's what I'm saying. I mean, it's perfectly understandable that you would want to take her upstairs, Theo.

I wasn't trying to take her anywhere, Theo said. She's her own person.

Sure, and her person is so nice you might like to take it upstairs and try to make another person.

You know what, Margot said. I think I'll go for that walk. She wobbled onto her feet, and everyone was silent as she dug for the flashlight. Her absence when she left was like an accusation against all three of them—Jesse for what he said, Issa for being beautiful, and Theo, for something he couldn't name but knew he was guilty of.

Aren't you going after her? he asked Jesse.

No, we've had this conversation before.

He looked sheepishly at Issa and hung his head like a bag on a pole.

She probably just needs a minute, Issa said.

She reached her tiny paw into the jar of lychees and pulled one out, the pale pink flesh dredging against the glass wall of the jar. When she opened her mouth and dipped her head back, Theo thought—*That's not for you.*

I'm just gonna go check on her, Theo said.

He caught up to Margot before the beach, and when he did she turned and it seemed like she had been expecting him. But without enthusiasm. This humbled him and made it easier to like her. The swishing of their jeans was identical, and the approaching ocean drowned it out little by little. The flashlight pointed far enough ahead that they were invisible to each other, and knowing it, Theo's face would not stop smiling. But that stopped once they stepped onto the sand and, the trees no longer blocking the moonlight, they could see each other again. Margot ended the silence, but her voice shunted like a car in traffic.

Can I ask you something? she said. They took off their shoes and walked toward the water. He wished she would be quiet and enjoy the oozing peace that was about to spread around both of them. It would pin them down like bees flooded in a pool of their own honey, their wings no longer theirs, surrendered ambition, stillness without the possibility of action.

He startled when she spoke again—a jumble of sounds that tumbled toward him and didn't become words until the sound stopped.

Why do you want to stay here so bad? was what Theo heard all at once.

I don't answer questions like that, he said.

And to prevent the inevitable follow-up, he spoke again out of turn: Questions where the person asking already thinks they know the answer.

She doesn't love you, Theo.

She's starting to.

With other people, you wouldn't have to make them. They just would. Naturally. On their own.

Good for them.

She looked down, turned her shoulders away from him and took a few paces to the left. When the tide reached Theo's feet, it felt freezing for a moment, but it was only in his head. It was as warm as always.

Now let *me* ask *you* something, he said. How come you haven't told anybody what you did to get sent to tsunami camp?

Because I didn't do anything.

Okay.

I just saw on the news how bad it was, and I asked my dad if I could go.

Really, said Theo, pushing forward, ready to pounce. So how is it that you feel so called by this tragedy that you come halfway around the world, and then as soon as you meet a couple of losers, you just throw it out the window and move with them to a bird house?

Her face toppled, but only for a second.

Kind of like how you dragged us all out here so you could hold onto Issa and now you're chasing me into the woods?

His face burned, but not because she was right.

Don't flatter yourself, he said. I'm here because you made everybody feel sorry for you, and I'm the nicest person out of three.

Fine, she said. So let's go back.

And just as Theo's anger was mounting, he felt what he thought was her foot brush up against his, her skin, smooth and colder than the water, jarringly intimate. He softened, and suddenly wanted not just to ask, but to know, how Margot had come to be here with them.

I asked you a question, he said.

He thought, or hoped, she would say: I don't answer questions like that. Meaning that, just as he suspected, he was the reason she had given up her mission and run away with them to the swiftlet house. That he had always been the one she cared about, even when she thought it was Jesse. But that isn't what she said. Instead, she said nothing, and when Theo closed his eyes briefly to deal privately with the sting of her silence, he was relieved to feel her cool foot on his once again. But when he opened his eyes, she was nowhere near him.

He looked down and screamed.

Margot came back then and pointed the flashlight at what first seemed like a bloated, whale-grey sea-creature, even despite its clothes. They stood—Margot's cheek pushed up against Theo's chest, his nails digging into her arm—looking at it for a long time, at her, what was left of her: a decomposing corpse. Its skin was so stretched from waterlog that the teeth showed, disturbingly small and widely spaced. The eyes had fallen out, or maybe they had been eaten. Stuck between the sand and the automatic door of the lapping waves, she rocked out a bed for herself. They could not stop watching until Theo finally decided it was enough and pried Margot away.

Wandering back toward the general direction of the house must have taken an hour because they kept losing direction or sitting down for a rest. Just as they were about to cross into the forest, Margot crossed her ankles and sunk into a seat, pulling Theo down by the hand with her.

What? he said.

He sat down next to her and felt the moisture of the dirt seep into his pants. He put his hand on her back and rubbed for several minutes without saying anything. He thought they might kiss, but they didn't.

We can't tell them about this, Margot finally said.

Why not?

Margot tilted her head, and her disappointment was like a firefly he wanted to catch before it went out again.

Forget it. Forget I said that. Of course I know why.

Margot nodded.

Good.

The next morning Theo found a bird in a low corner of the closet. But it was not the gray kind with the alien head he was used to seeing, the kind that this house was built to lure. It was a swallow, the kind of common creature—like a squirrel or raccoon—it was surprising to see in exotic places. It had probably come into the house by mistake. He came closer and saw something in its beak that looked familiar. A fleck of red marbled with brown. It was a lychee rind from the pile he had discarded behind the house.

Foamy water lapped into the corpse's open mouth over and over again as Theo scanned Issa for her reaction. They had come to the beach that morning the same as the last twenty-three mornings. Theo had been worried about being convincing in front of her and Jesse that they were all seeing the body for the first time, but he needn't have worried. Issa stared blankly for several minutes then suggested moving far enough down the beach to be invisible in case a clean-up crew showed up. Margot stood back from the others to hide her face going bright red.

After walking a satisfying distance, they put their blankets down and talked for a while; no one felt like swimming. Jesse said it had looked exactly like a body he pulled out of a collapsed doorway in Aceh. Issa said maybe she had gotten tossed back and it was the same person washed up here. Jesse laughed, and so did Theo. Margot said nothing the whole time, but Theo could feel her waiting for Issa and Jesse to leave them in privacy. When they finally decided to swim, her breathy gratefulness came flowing out.

Can you believe them? she said quickly, not wanting to waste a second of privacy. Making jokes about this.

They've seen a lot of drowned bodies, Theo said in a cold monotone, not looking at her. So have I. So have you. It's not like there's anything to do about it.

Come on, Theo. I was there last night. Even when we were sitting in the forest, you were still in shock. You could barely speak, you were shaking, and that was like half an hour after.

He believed her so tried to remember shaking but couldn't. Maybe she had just wanted to remind him that they had shared something in the forest, so he wouldn't forget her for Issa, but it wasn't working. He had been moved in the forest, too, but now she was just ruining it by forcing it in his face. For this reason and others, he wished she would stop talking, but she didn't. He looked down at his book. His finger marked the page he'd left off reading, and his eye-line scurried alongside the words like an insect. He barely listened as Margot talked, and in fact was doing a good job of blocking out the whole physical world, until a shadow floated above his head and a droplet of ocean water splashed on the back of his calf. He looked up and saw its source—Issa's sopping hair. She was standing behind him. Margot's head dropped, and when Theo straightened himself and Issa flipped herself over his shoulder and toppled into his lap, laughing as she soaked him, Margot slunk away to the water to join Jesse.

That night, Theo suffered Jesse's snore, which was even more annoying for being barely audible so forcing you to listen for it. Theo went downstairs and in the dark, reached into the snoring. Luckily, he caught Margot's elbow. Later she told him she had been fully awake with her eyes open and would have helped if she knew what he was doing. He pulled her to her feet and led her up to the roof, not having made any decision to act but just acting. This was not like him. He did not even bring his satchel of condoms.

On the roof, they barely even whispered, first because they were terrified of getting caught, and then because they didn't need to. But when they said goodnight, the calm vanished and he walked to his bed in a panic about what he had done—how if Issa found out, she might not even care but would leave him anyway. Lying down, he focused all his energy on calming his breathing. Eventually he coaxed himself to sleep, but it was not for long. He dreamt about the time his father took him to a waterpark in central Florida, where he spent the day bobbing in a gargantuan wave-pool, emerging every half-hour when the siren came on to wait out the storm of waves, which scared him. In the dream, the siren neglected to sound, and the waves started before he could get to the shallow end.

Each of the next three nights, Theo was back to the roof with Margot. On the fourth, he waited for her as he had done previously, but she didn't come. He crouched on the stairs and could hear her whispering with Jesse. The next morning as the others were inspecting their areas and getting ready to leave for the beach, Theo pulled Margot aside. He planned to tell her that it was over between them. But before he had a chance, she netted him with explanation.

I'm so sorry about last night, she said. He wouldn't go to sleep.

He must have slept eventually.

Well yes, but not until really late, and I figured you'd be sleeping?

It's no big deal, Margot. Relax.

I'll come up tonight. I promise.

Whatever.

At the beach, Issa started drinking earlier than usual. She gathered her legs to one side and sat on her towel, golden hair catching sparks. She challenged Jesse to a race and when she beat him, she took her top off and twirled with her towel whipping around her. She grabbed both of Theo's hands and pulled him up to his feet.

Let's swim, she said.

He nodded and stood up to remove his shirt. She jumped on his back to be carried to the water, fiddling with the money pouch around his neck. He closed his eyes to the warm belly against his back, squeezed both of her thighs in his palms, and walked into the ocean. He crouched down, and the water flowed in between them. She floated away, but clung to him and pulled herself back. She must have suspected things between him and Margot. Not consciously maybe, but on some level, she knew. And maybe, it occurred to him, it would actually work to his advantage. But then he made the mistake of testing the theory.

Do you love me? he said.

She laughed and pushed her hand into his pants.

Come on, I'm serious.

I do, she said.

I love you.

And I love *you*, she said, but it was through clenched teeth. Theo pushed his feet to the ground and when he stood up, was surprised that the water barely reached his waist. He thought he had brought them out deeper.

That evening, Theo went for a long walk and missed dinner. When he got back, Margot was waiting outside for him, looking angry.

I came upstairs this morning after inspection, she whispered. And I found two fragments that had obviously been building for more than a day.

Really?

Yeah, really. So since when are you so careless?

Take it easy.

I am taking it easy. You went from hall monitor to slacker as soon as we started sleeping together. Tell me how not to take that personally. Don't you want to stay here as long as possible? I do. I can't even think about what it will be like for me when I have to leave you.

He pushed her hair off her face and pretended to be sympathetic, but in reality, he floated above her vulnerability not like a plane—in a different atmosphere, going somewhere definitive, meaning business—but more like a blimp—still nearby and in view but also out of reach, moving only at the speed of time.

Me too, he said.

It was a couple of afternoons later that they returned from the beach to two messengers dawdling outside the house next to a pile of their booted luggage. Theo, approaching first, switched directions and called out to the others to run, which they did with urgency, but the guards gave no chase. When they realized they were running from no one, they stopped and watched from a distance the messengers tear apart their luggage, taking for themselves whatever interested them, especially the money. Theo patted his chest.

When the men left, they counted to a hundred and went to appraise what was left of their stuff. Margot knelt to sift through the rubble. Issa lit a cigarette and lifted a pair of Jesse's boxers with her toe, but for once Jesse didn't laugh. He avoided her gaze and moved toward Margot.

Here's what we'll do, Jesse said, not looking at anyone. We'll go into town. We'll get a hotel room for the night. Theo still has money. Tomorrow, maybe we scope out some other bird houses.

Right, Theo said. Theo still has money.

And I'm sure Theo will share it with everyone else who just got robbed and is stranded in the woods, Margot said.

Theo ignored her. Even so, the nest people are obviously back to work as usual, right? He pointed to the pile of their luggage. We could find another house, but we'll be right back here again, a couple of days tops.

I'm not going back to that camp, Jesse said. Right? Margot?

I doubt they would take us back anyway, she mumbled and wound her thin arms around her torso.

I know you two aren't, Jesse said to Theo and Issa. So the only question is, are the four of us staying together or not?

Theo, Issa said. Can I talk to you in private?

She walked toward the tree where a few lychee rinds still remained of the ones Theo had scattered.

I wasn't going to say anything because what was the point, she said. But you were right. Jesse stole a bunch of money from me. There's no way I could trust him to go somewhere else with him.

He expected to feel relieved to finally hear her accuse him. After all the laughing he had endured. The drinking and friendship. Her covering up the money. But he did not feel relieved, and she could tell.

Feel free to stick by them if that's your truth, Issa said. I'll be good on my own.

Theo shook his head.

No.

Cool, said Issa. I'm glad.

They walked back to the house with arms draped around each other. Margot tried to make him look at her, but he was already too far away. She would have to deal with it on her own. With Issa, he kneeled to gather the rest of their scattered belongings, and stuffed them into their bags.

Check to make sure you don't have anything of theirs, he told Issa.

What are you doing? Jesse said, but Theo didn't feel obligated to answer.

Theo! Margot said.

A low scream started in him then that was full of anguish and guilt and love, but it was still miles away then and no one could hear it. Especially not Margot, and barely even Theo. He pushed shirts and towels and sneakers into his bag and refused to look up. Margot tried Issa instead.

You know he did this on purpose, she said, tears creeking down her face. Theo helped Issa hoist her pack onto one shoulder, then the next. Neither of them paid any attention to what Margot was saying. Why do you think he suddenly stopped being so fucking paranoid about everything? Huh? He wanted to get thrown out. Ask him why!

Theo reached into his money pouch and took out a twenty, held it out to Jesse.

That should get you through the night. Tomorrow you'll have to call your parents.

Jesse snatched the money out of his hand but said nothing. Theo and Issa turned and started toward town. Sobbing, Margot ran into the house and up the steps. The horrendous sound of her wailing was audible to Theo and Issa for longer than would seem possible as they moved through the forest.

LURE

DERICK MATTERN

the cormorants dive in and out of us tonight
catching words as they dart and squirm
I've seen bays illumined by nets of bulbs
jigging for squid seen swarms of electric
blue ones cast the light that catches them
they say if you've hooked one you've caught
its mate tonight the city lights have gone out
and our lines drift toward tangling in the
dark

THE CARPET-BAG: *MOBY DICK* CHAPTER 2

JESSICA CUELLO

Like a candle in a tomb,
a boy seeks a bed: free,
alone. We keep inside—

our bodies cannot move
on streets or boats.
It's unseemly.

We cannot be alone.
We cannot without a man.
We were born to keep

in walls and if we dream
of space, we must
be falling. In our minds

we map the layout
of the walls. Our limbs
move by tasks not will.

We were born in bed—
born to imitate,
hands made to clench.

We bring water.
Then silence, a baby.
We rock and feed,

tethered to our fathers,
to the others.
We never wander.

"Untitled" by George Davis Cathcart

CONFESSION

Barbara Abramson

They say that Matthew is on the street, so I avoid the street. I don't want to see him, or hear him, or smell him, either, as he is now, if they are to be believed. And I do believe them, although they always did exaggerate where he was concerned. Now they talk about him more than ever. They're "trying to understand." I could explain—possibly. Certainly, I could add something to the discussion. But in my own crummy way—not that it matters—I'm loyal.

The last time I saw Matthew was in early November: a cold iron sky, the air thick with bitter damp. People shuffled along the street like so many shackled prisoners under the weight of their coats and scarves and failing boots. I had dragged myself out of Robarts Library about three o'clock in a red-eyed stupefaction of overwork, anxiety, and boredom, so I almost walked right past Matthew when he stopped me. I admit I felt flattered that he even recognized me.

He was ridiculously handsome even with his face slapped red by the cold, but his loose black Bacchus curls looked unwashed, and he hadn't shaved in two or three days. Normally he came to class looking like an ad for something really expensive, like an actor ready for glaring lights and enthralling close-ups.

"Everyone is still so surprised that you left the program," I said. He'd dropped out without a word to anyone, and just when he'd won another grant.

"I just couldn't see the point of doing a Master's degree anymore. I needed a change. Right now I'm working at the Hog's Head." He gestured at the red brick building across the street. Beneath its sign a marquee read, *Get drunk where your father did.* The place was so shabby even students found it depressing; it was more of a venue for committed losers.

"You work *there*? Are you thinking of going into social work?"

He laughed. "It's temporary. I'm thinking about going to law school. Or architecture. Or something else. I'm thinking over my options."

The world is my oyster, he didn't say aloud, because he didn't need to. There is nothing I can say that could exaggerate his reputation, or my disappointment when I finally got to share a class with him. When he spoke, which wasn't often, everyone, including the professor, would lean forward, breath held, and I would lean with them. But what he had to say was always crushingly ordinary, and worse, delivered in the grave, humorless manner of someone imparting highly valuable information. He once said—no, *intoned*—"History is written by the winners," as if it had never been said before. I remember the long moment of respectful silence that followed these words. I remember the other students nodding to each other wisely, and the professor taking a deep, satisfied breath and smiling. I found it mystifying. Was I really superior to them all, or was I just insensible? Why was I the only one who couldn't see this star shining?

"A couple of the profs called me afterward and tried to talk me into coming back. I was their great white hope."

Their great white hope?—but I didn't dare laugh. It was true. I'd whiled away the boring parts of many seminars, concocting impossible schemes to read his work without actually having to come out and ask—I didn't want to be one more of the many feeding his vanity until he exploded.

"Well, let's be honest—not everyone is sorry," I said. "The really competitive ones are relieved."

"So you're relieved." He wasn't being sarcastic. It was just another statement of what he called fact, in that solemn, self-regarding manner I found so maddening in class.

"Me? I'm not competitive. You must be confusing me with someone else. I bet you don't even know my name."

"You're Marian."

What more did I want? I should have stopped there. Instead, I asked him if he had time for a coffee—it was one last chance to ask to read his priceless essays. I wasn't afraid of my invitation being misunderstood: the other students saw me as a kind of visiting zoo animal rather than a peer. I was married, and I was old. Matthew had been there the day I'd announced that it was my thirtieth birthday. He couldn't seem to get past the horror of it any better than I could. That was probably why he'd remembered my name.

Matthew's first polite questions when we sat down were about my husband. We each took a turn praising his generosity and patience for allowing me to give up my job "just to pursue such a worthless prize," as Matthew said repeatedly, as a Master's degree in history.

We'd entered the Second Cup during one of its rare interludes of quiet. When he took off his coat I could see he'd grown noticeably thinner than when I'd last seen him, the magnetic center of the classroom, his body emanating a kind of subcutaneous…something, issuing alerts to our skin.

He draped our coats over chairs at the tables on either side of us, to make them look occupied. "I don't like to be crowded," he said.

I suppose I did crowd him, that I conducted an interrogation rather than a conversation. Matthew had an articulate, pompous, and poorly considered theory on just about everything: current European literary theory, the semiology of Mussolini's Jewish mistress, the rising occurrence of anorexia.

"Youth and beauty were not always commodities," he said. "They weren't always worshipped the way they are now."

"That is absolute nonsense," I said. I felt strangely free to be unpleasant; I only held back the word 'disingenuous' because of the compliment it implied. "Give me one shred of evidence for that statement. It's human nature to be attracted to those things."

"There is no such thing as human nature. Even modes of personal interaction have changed over time. People didn't talk so much in former times."

"How on earth do you know that?"

"Well…"

"It would be an interesting idea if there were any verifiable way for you to prove it. What would you consider to be evidence for a statement like that? Where would you go to find it?"

He laughed a little. "You're right," he said, shrugged, and smiled. That smile, unexpectedly and endearingly crooked, higher on the left, cancelled out the complacent shrug that should have been so infuriating. Then he reached across into his coat pocket and pulled out a pack of cigarettes.

"Not *here*," I said like a fool, pointing to the No Smoking sign, as if I could hear the police sirens already. He smiled at me again, full on, and I made the mistake of looking at him, really looking at him. It was a face that kept the eye moving delightedly back and forth across the soft geometry of its structure, from the dense black eyebrows almost hidden below his bangs to his aquiline nose, the bridge of it a broken diamond; from his reddened prominent cheekbones to his square jaw; from the bruise-blue hollows below his eyes to the single dimple in his right cheek. His large round eyes, as beautiful and pure of white as a child's, which I had lazily thought of as dark, were in fact coffee-brown, the irises shattered by spots and splinters of gold. His hands, now pressed against the table top, had the hairy knuckles I so dislike on most men. I realized I was leaning in a little too closely. He didn't seem to notice, or anyway, to begrudge me. He was used to it, after all. I am ordinary, I thought, and just for that one moment, I didn't even resent it. I'd found him so boring, so disappointing, but I was wrong; I realized it was wonderful that he would even bother to work, and study, and strive, too, when all he had to do was let us look at him.

"I mean…I didn't know you smoked. I didn't know vegetarians were…*allowed* to."

"I used to when I was a kid. I guess I started again when I started work." He nodded in the direction of the Hog's Head, and stared worriedly at the building as if he'd left something essential there. I assumed he was getting ready to leave; I couldn't believe he had spent this long with me. He still kept the fingers of both hands pressed down on the table top between us, the nail beds gone white with the pressure, resisting the call of the cigarette.

"I just can't picture you there," I said.

"If you were a real tyrant," he said, smiling wonderfully, "and not just a wannabe, what morally reprehensible law would you pass? It's a game I like to play. I mean a law that in reality you would never permit, something you're ashamed of yourself for wanting?"

"Easy. I wouldn't allow any girl to marry a man a lot older than her. I know a lot of those couples imagine they're in love, but really, the girls are selling themselves, and the men are buying them, and it shouldn't be allowed. I wouldn't care if it was just sex, but those people are buying and selling love, and it shouldn't be allowed."

All this had poured out, somehow, before I realized how it might sound. Ten years difference at the most, I would say when Matthew asked, and explain that my father had been fifteen years older than my mother and treated her like a child. I was also quite prepared to lie and tell him that my husband, Dan, was only four years older than I was, or the truth—ten years older—or even say 'just joking'—because I was joking. If Dan and I had been born in the very same hour, the problems would have been the same.

But Matthew didn't ask. Instead he leaned halfway across the table and sneered at me, and he wasn't beautiful anymore. "Oh, yes, that's right," he said, his face pinched with contempt, "as if love weren't just a commodity like any other. Yeah, right, sex is nothing—you feel cool being able to say that—but love...love is *holy*. And pretending you actually believe that makes *you* feel holy."

He'd finally said something I'd never heard before. I was relieved, if insulted. I felt excited, too, because at least the game had gotten interesting.

"Why? What morally reprehensible law would you pass?"

"There's lots of unconscionable laws," he said, frowning, turning his empty mug around and around in his hands. "The British had a law making attempted suicide punishable by death. But I guess *you* already knew that." He seemed to be aiming his sarcasm at someone else; he wasn't even looking at me. "I'll tell you something," Matthew said. "I've had three friends commit suicide. After they were dead, I just stopped caring about them." He snapped his fingers. "Just like that."

I knew what I was supposed to say—that of course he'd cared, and that he shouldn't be ashamed of such tender feelings. But I couldn't help myself.

"*Three?* Really, three? Were you working at one of those help centres?"

"I left home when I was seventeen. I went to Montreal to play bass with a rock band. I got to know all sorts of people. The sort of people my parents had never even heard of." He put his mug aside on the next table. "A couple of them were male prostitutes. And they were happy like that." He turned away from me, and his eyes fixed on space. "They were happy like that. They were. It was their choice. But by the time they hit their mid-twenties, they felt they were starting to lose their looks. And you know, this one guy, he had the kind of body Michelangelo only *wished* David had."

Matthew's face became expressionless, and he did something very strange; he pulled his elbows up stiff and high behind him, forcing his shoulders up almost to his ears. "And this guy felt really guilty about being gay, and his psychiatrist and his friends and the support groups and the action groups kept telling him he shouldn't feel guilty, but there was just no way this guy could accept that. And one day, this guy just cut it off. And he lived."

It? Oh, *it*. Or maybe I said this aloud. I don't know.

"You have to feel sorry for a guy like that," he said, all the time rising very slowly from his chair—being pulled up, it seemed, by his elbows—rising up so slowly I remembered the slow-motion sensation of falling from the tree where I'd been trying to rescue our cat, Sable. I was fifteen; I should have known much, much better. The ground seemed to take forever to meet me.

"I've always had a silver spoon in my mouth. I've always had things easy. Even those two years when I should have been starving, I did fine. I did just fine." By now he'd risen six inches above his chair and just stood, frozen there. His knees were locked at an angle, and his arms seemed to be pinioned high behind him. Whatever he was about to say next was dangling him like a puppet. He was strangling, but his face and voice remained smooth and untroubled, nonchalant. He was oblivious to the grotesque mime he was performing. That was worse for me than anything else.

Why me? I thought, as if a doctor had just told me I was going to die. I knew what Matthew was going to say, and that I absolutely didn't want to hear it. *Why me?* I felt truly frantic. *No, no, please don't say it, just don't;* and it may be that death is simply more knowledge than any one person can live with. Why didn't I stop him? Not *here*, I should have said. Sit down, I should have said, sit down, Matthew—but I said nothing. I was afraid to wake this sleepwalker poised to fall off the edge. And I couldn't really believe what was happening. And to be honest, I felt flattered. I thought Matthew was confiding in me.

"No, I certainly didn't starve. I did fine," he said calmly, and something wrenched his elbows back so hard I thought they would break.

Because he got a phone call he saw a picture an obituary because I said the wrong thing I goaded him because he saw someone in the street in this room that he used to know because he is having a nervous breakdown because I'm special because I'm nobody. Because I'm nobody.

"When you're young and white and good-looking in Montreal, there's always someone to look after you. Always. There were always rich men to take care of me."

It was done. His arms fell to his sides; he straightened up, blinked a few times, and slid back into his chair, still staring at nothing. Then he moved his gaze back in my direction and more or less looked at me.

I can't remember what I said next, if anything. If only I had said, 'So what?' That's what I wanted to say. That's what I should have said. But I was afraid that if I opened my mouth to speak, my body might betray me, too. I racked my little arsenal of stock phrases for something truly empty to say. It was only polite to pretend that nothing had happened. From his dazed look, I wasn't sure that he even knew that anything had.

But he must have known some of it; he began talking about his girlfriend, Sandra. He lived with Sandra, his girlfriend, and living with his girlfriend Sandra wasn't easy. Sandra left her clothes lying around their bedroom. Sandra never made any real effort when it was her turn to make dinner. Sandra would just pop out her contact lens when there was something in it and lick it clean, a really disgusting habit, and not just for a girlfriend.

I nodded, I nodded; I nodded as if both our lights might go out if I stopped. I knew I should oblige him by complaining, in turn, about my husband's irritating habits—his faults, his failures, even his betrayals—but now I couldn't remember even one from the long list I'd thought permanently inscribed on my heart.

"The time is 5:30," the radio announcer said, and I realized the radio had been playing in the background all along. There had been other people in the café all along. It must have filled and emptied at least twice since we'd come in. I wondered how many other people had seen the beautiful man lose control.

"I'm sorry, I have to go home and make dinner," I said. "It's always my turn."

We put on our coats and walked to the door together. It was already dark, and a punishing rain was falling, an iron-fisted rain. I told Matthew my car wasn't far away, and politely offered him a lift.

"But I'm sure you have to go straight home," he said in a mocking tone. "Don't go out of your way just for me."

It's absurd for me to feel guilty, and it's conceited, and it's unfair. What difference could I possibly have made? Matthew sounded angry. I thought he was angry at me, just as a little boy will kick the stone that tripped him. So to reassure him that nothing had happened, that I did not feel closer to him or presume that now we were friends, to show him that nothing had changed, I said yes, I had to go straight home, and I just left him there.

CLING

DERICK MATTERN

even in winter the vines hold fast
come summer the trellis will shade
my window from the street below but
on these early evenings stranded as
coal smoke twines among alleyways
every fog-bright shape could be yours

PHOTO ALBUM

GLENN FREEMAN

Here is the inhabited kingdom, the blind
metaphor, horse-drawn carriages in
the park, light on broken glass. A bitter wind
howls down avenues I've never seen.
Fond memories of moments that disappear
like light across a canvas, the memory
and the moment side by side. No one lives here
anymore; no design controls the scene.
Peeling paint. Dust in the corners. Owls roost
in the maple boughs; vines crawl up the white
walls in an Instagram haze: each produced
memory unfolds into fuzzy light.
There are always leaves on the ground; always
sunlight misted into haze, mirrors blurred into doorways.

Blue

Kristen MacKenzie

My dad went into the Air Force when he was in his early twenties, joining just in time to become an airplane mechanic in Vietnam. To hear him tell it, his time spent there was more of an exotic vacation than a job. There were stories about the bizarre things served in local restaurants and about the pranks airmen played on each other. He held dozens of slides up to the light over the dining room table, showing us tiny, bright windows into a green, completely foreign world. His blunt fingertip would trace the edges of the slide that held the one image of himself, unrecognizable with his soft face and uniform, standing alongside a battered little aircraft.

Whenever we were outside and the sound of an engine roared overhead, he would pause and put his head to the side a little, closing one eye and listening.

"Cessna 172," he'd say with a slow smile that hinted at secrets from a time before he was a father and a Bible salesman.

When I was thirteen, I watched *Top Gun* for the first time. I was sick in bed with the flu, and Mom rented it as a special treat. We had moved from eastern Washington that summer, leaving behind a house in the country where we each had our own room and forty acres out back to roam, to a dingy duplex in one of the low-rent suburbs of Seattle where my sister and I shared a bedroom. We arrived SeaFair weekend knowing nothing about hydroplane races, the parade, or the airshows. When I saw dog-fighting F-14s on the little screen of our television, and heard the growl of real live jets overhead, I forgot I was sick. I forgot about the house in the country and the friends we left behind. I forgot I'd wanted to become a doctor. I forgot I was a girl. I wanted to be Maverick and fly jets.

By the time I hit my twenties, I'd begun dating a Navy corpsman and moved out to Whidbey Island to live with him, only a few miles away from the Naval Air Station that was home to the kind of planes that made enough noise, they would've kept my dad smiling for a week. This was pre-9/11 and in those days, civilians were allowed on base after having presented the gate with a valid driver's license and being given a temporary pass. On lunch break from my job at the YMCA, I would drive to the end of the runway and park alongside the chain link fence, watching the EA-6B Prowlers take off and land. I could feel the roar of the engines, so loud and so big my body, my mind, would give in and let go of the clutter that seemed to weigh me down. I would drive away feeling emptied out, clean and clear.

When the relationship with the corpsman was over, I moved to a tiny yellow house perched at the edge of a field with only a fringe of fir trees between me and the beach. I was not alone for long. For the past eighteen months, my daughter had lived with my mom to give me the chance to pull myself together after a failed marriage, but it was time for her to be home again, whether or not either of us was ready. She arrived late one night a few weeks after I'd settled in. The husband I'd left behind drove her across the state in his old blue truck, expertly packed with all of the things that make up a little girl's bedroom.

The truck rumbled up the gravel drive, accelerating to keep from stalling on the sharp grade, back tires spinning under the weight of the load it carried. My gut felt as heavy as all the things I could see under the tarp in the truck's bed as it came to a stop.

I heard my ex-husband's voice inside the cab, speaking with his usual patience to my daughter.

"Sable, put your shoes on first." Her reply was lost in the sound of her door slamming shut. Shoes could clearly wait.

She had grown; of course she had. She still looked smaller than the other first-graders I worked with at the daycare center, shoulders narrow under the straps of her pack. Her hair was fuzzing over her ears just as mine did, only pale blond where mine was brown. Her face was lit by the light falling from the living room window, and her little fingers were gripped tight on the handle of her bulging Pocahontas backpack.

Joe paused in the doorway after letting go of Sable's hand. My eyes measured him against the frame of the door and I felt a sense of shock, recognizing he was only a few inches taller than I was. Somehow, he'd always seemed bigger. I watched his face shifting through emotion and could tell he was trying to decide whether to comment on my choice of music. The name of the song was "Break Stuff," and calling it music was stretching it. It was childish, rubbing his face in my complete departure from the role of Christian wife and mother, but I didn't turn it off.

If Sable had any reaction to the music, or to her new home, I don't remember it. In fact, I don't remember much at all about the rest of our first night together again, except my ex-husband's offer to pray for me as he left. I didn't take him up on it.

My days took on a very different shape after Sable's return home. She came with me to work at the daycare, and melted into the group of schoolchildren invisibly, doing as she was told, never speaking up, and moving along like a little blue-eyed robot, while I watched from the toddler room where I taught. She was not the same child I'd said good-bye to a year and a half ago.

At night, all of the things that had funneled into her during the day, silently absorbed, seem to come out in garbled messages, meltdowns that would pitch her into self-destructive fits, smashing her fists and sometimes even her head against her bedroom door. All that seemed to stop them was wrapping myself around her like an octopus and holding tight until she stopped struggling. When she fell asleep, I would go outside and sit on the hood of my car in the gravel drive, hug my knees to my chest, and listen to the roar of the jets across the bay. I closed my eyes and tracked them across the sky, measuring my heartbeat in the silence between, ignoring the tears.

I used to put on my running shoes and fly over the wooded trails of Ft. Ebey State Park, soundless as the bats that swooped through dark hollows between the trees on either side of me. The sun would set while I stood on the beach, breathing salt off the water and steam from my body as the air cooled around me. All of that ended when Sable returned. If I saw the sun set, it was through the trees, stolen glimpses caught from her bedroom window as we fought. Her voice would take on that sullen note that instantly made my hands go into fists, and it didn't matter what she said—the usual argument about staying up later, or having one more snack—it was everything I could do to keep from slamming her door and walking away from the house.

"Dad would let me," she would often say to conclude the argument, raising her chin at me with a look that was her father, through and through. I would fix my eyes on the dull shine of the metal screen in her windows and try to imagine it made me a good mother, that I didn't answer to that retort.

On a day that was rare for the Washington coast, still and heavy with not a cloud in the sky, I gave up mid-battle. The horizon was fading into a fallen-down rainbow, crimson on the water, blackberry-blue up high where the first stars were beginning to poke through the dark, and the pull to be out there in the middle of it stopped me partway through a threat.

"This isn't working, is it?" I asked her, and she stopped crying and looked at me, wordless.

"Do you want to get out of here?" I said, and she did.

It wasn't the end to all battles, but it was the start of something hopeful, the two of us running over darkening trails, splashing rocks into ocean sunsets, and racing barefoot across the Deception Pass bridge, ignoring our fear of heights and of each other. Because we *were* both afraid, I saw; she was afraid of being sent away again and I was afraid of not being able to care for her. They were very real possibilities.

Only weeks after she arrived, an argument in the car that went on and on pushed me to my snapping point as we got closer to home, and all I wanted was to be alone again. I parked the car along the rail at the pass and ordered her to stay inside, locking the door and slamming it shut.

The wind was cold on my face and I stood for a long time, letting my eyes go blurry watching the green rush of water under the bridge rail, the dizzy black swirl of eddies. I went back when my hands had stopped shaking, but the car was empty.

The shaking began again. Only a month earlier, a child had been lost here, and his body had never been recovered. I thought of the vicious pull of the current and started running back the length of the bridge, calling her name, remembering with a jolt high up in my chest my earlier desire to be alone.

"Not like this, please, not like this."

"Ma'am?" The man and woman across the road shouted over the noise of traffic.

My daughter hid behind them, pressed against the thin metal wires of the suspension railing, not looking at me. The rush of relief made my leg bones feel hollowed out and filled again with jelly but it was anger that got me over the rail and across the road, dodging a passing truck. They surrendered her to me with obvious reluctance. When I turned my head to check for traffic, they were watching us still.

Summer was over quickly, and our favorite trails were muddy wallows. A new coffee shop had opened in town and our nightly escapes turned to weekly trips for the treat of a hot caramel apple cider before bedtime. It became a favorite hangout for the unmarried Naval officers as well, and before long, I met a pilot. We weren't dating more than a few weeks before I realized it wasn't so much that I wanted to be with this man; I wanted to *be* him.

"Tell me what it feels like when you lift off," I'd say, pushing out of his embrace to watch his face as he described the sudden feeling of weight on his chest, the rush of adrenaline through his legs that felt like ants crawling. His words made my blood go faster. His kisses did not.

We parted amicably and the pile of books on my nightstand changed from romance novels to aviation history and little glossy books with pictures of planes that were my version of porn. I spent my lunch breaks memorizing the load capacity, maximum speed, and G-force rating of the EA-6B Prowler. At night, I began doing shaky pushups and jumping jacks that shook the old floorboards of the living room, pretending it was possible for a 25-year-old nearsighted single mother to join the Navy and fly fighter jets. The realities were hard to ignore for long though, and the workouts continued. But the books went back to the library, along with my hopes for a different sort of life. Sometimes my daughter sat with me after dark on the hood, both of us silent and bundled up, listening to the airplanes in the distance.

We made it a few years, she and I, island times with equal parts argument and adventure, before it became clear she needed more than I could give. Her father took her to live with him, and no one spoke of regret. I moved to the city. I wasn't alone for long. Ten years passed and I didn't hear the jets or run through the woods to the shore. Arguments and adventures were fit into weekends and my daughter grew up.

She called me when she turned eighteen, and told me she was going into the Air Force. I didn't remember the books on my nightstand or the sound of a jet as it turned its wings to the sun and growled at the edge of the horizon. All I saw were headlines, soldiers traded for democracy in someone else's country. I thought of blonde hair bloodied and blue eyes that wouldn't open again. There were no arguments; she just stopped calling.

That summer felt like it would flatten me, August bearing down like a sweaty fist. I hadn't forgotten the date; I knew the jets would fly over me as they did most every year. I went walking to have them overhead with no roof between, to let them clear away the clutter, to lift me up a bit, just as they had before. The streets were mid-morning quiet; not even a lawnmower covered up the birdcalls and then even those went away.

A jet performing or destroying is gone by the time its sound wraps around you and shakes loose the barrier between you and the sky. The noise of six jets ripping across the space above silent suburbia landed on me like a sledgehammer, pounding me into disconnected pieces. I don't remember walking back to the house, only the image, clearer than anything else in front of me, of the jet in the lead coming down in an arc through the fringe of maple leaves above my head and straight through me, splitting me in half. And I wanted it. I barricaded myself in, windows shut against the sound, locked in the deepest part of the house while they passed overhead again and again, shaking the walls, covering up the noise of a full-grown woman wailing like a child.

The sound that once had been medicine to me was now the sound of itself, without my dreams to give it form. My illusion was stripped and so was I, bare and frightened. It wasn't freedom I was hearing, or escape. It was a machine and a man, built to make people feel just as I did in that moment, built to destroy. And my daughter was becoming a part of that.

She graduated with the rest of them, hundreds all the same, her hat held in shaky hands, afraid to stand out in any way. She tried not to cry when she saw us, both parents in the same place, but she failed. There was no mascara to smear when she wiped her eyes. Camouflage hides tears. I was proud, even if I'd never wanted this, not for what she was part of, but for who she'd become.

When she calls me now, she tells me how many months she has left in the service, and they stretch out far ahead. Her new neighbor in the dorms is a musician, she jokes bravely, and I hear the thump of drums and a cat-screech of guitar before she hangs up the phone. She isn't in Afghanistan. She hasn't been trained to kill. She hands out pills all day and gets her dental work for free. She talks about going to college when she's done.

When August comes next year, and the noise begins overhead, I won't be around to hear it. I'm going to be in the trees, where my footsteps don't make any sound and the shore is just ahead. I'll throw rocks until the bats come out and swoop across the sky, silent.

LOOKING AHEAD

JIM GUSTAFSON

The coefficient of monotony,
endless shore, endless sea, endless sky.
Right words rubbed create friction,
amble in smolder, slip in flames,
and drown reaching after moon arms.

What of the rest? There is no response.
The view is disrupted. What view isn't?
The desert, where you can see forever
finishes at the sky.

All things come in bottles.

THE COUNTERPANE: *MOBY DICK* CHAPTER 4

JESSICA CUELLO

Not his real mother,
I beat him supperless
and shut him in alone

I found him up the chimney
leaving me, because I haven't done
enough, not good enough

I beat because I can't see
and sit or breathe.
Children are a housekeeping

their tiny voices like a leak
a speaking floor that must shut up
a no that says yes

they're not even your own
with eyes from elsewhere
and a mind, a whine, trying

to get out of the attic room
trying to come back down
and get free: No one is. So

take your medicine. Sit down.
Take your four walls,
the moment when your arm

blends and the quilt begins—
when you end and the terror
visits. We live with it.

"Untitled" by George Davis Cathcart

THE GOOD SIDE OF THE WORLD

GEORGE L. CHIEFFET

At night when Zach walked beside the highway, he watched the solitary drivers, their headlights glowing out of the dark, and wondered where those cars were going and where they had come from. He imagined the drivers living in squat bungalows with attached carports and ragged, postage-stamp lawns. He saw each driver hunched over his steering wheel, peering through a smudged window at the narrow ribbon of highway leading to some distant place. He tried to imagine each of them driving off in the dark at four in the morning. He saw them all as young men with beard stubble and tobacco-stained fingernails. He imagined the offices and factories where they worked as tall, gray buildings decorated with marble lobbies and glowing lamps, or low-slung factory buildings of corrugated steel and concrete, tall smokestacks belching smoke, machines whirring under neon lights. Did these men feel the same pangs of loneliness he often felt? Alone every night in his rented room, Zach fantasized about Holly

Belcamp, the girl he watched from his window in the second-floor apartment across the street. Zach had only learned her name by accident from a piece of misplaced mail in his box. Otherwise, she was a mystery to him, a mystery he spied on at dusk when a lamp brightened her curtains, and, concealed behind a half-pulled drape, he squinted into his binoculars and aimed them in the direction of her bedroom. With her curtains closed and the bedroom light shining, he saw her silhouette floating across the fabric, glowing with a translucence that lent it an unworldly presence.

When her curtains were open, he might glimpse Holly preening in front of a full-length mirror, tweezing her brows and painting a dark purple on her lips, or sometimes merely sitting on her chair, its upholstered arms shaped like elephant ears, her long shapely legs folded across one armrest, a towel wrapped like a turban around her beautiful chestnut hair. While she watched TV and ate ice cream, her restless movements suggested that something was missing from her life. Zach wanted to pry open the window sash and call out to her.

But he refrained from doing so, being a tall and awkward young man with a long face and small, putty-colored eyes. He had always wanted to be a hero but knew he would never be one. He squinted down at his toes when he walked and often stuttered when he spoke, and, worst of all, he was fearful. He hid his money, stashing it in a footlocker under his bed, folding each ten-dollar bill in half and using a paper fastener to clip the bills together in wads. He brooded over his solitude. He lived in a sea of anxieties. When he had nothing to watch from his window, he crawled under his cot to search out the footlocker amidst the dust motes and stray socks. Sometimes he dreamed that a man under his bed waited to kill him. Sometimes he imagined himself as an old man dying in bed. Sometimes, late at night, his chin resting on the sill, he counted the stars one by one, sectioning the sky into quadrants, each quadrant a single pane of window glass. He counted until he lost patience because he was unable to distinguish the stars he had counted from the uncounted ones. He soon realized there were too many stars to count.

The tiny dormer window where he viewed the stars was the good side of the house, for on the other side, where the overhang of the garage roof darkened the large back window and blocked out the light, he watched the comings and goings of Tony Carhart. Carhart was an insurance salesman who drove an old convertible and sometimes dated Holly. During the evening, concealed behind his burlap window curtain, Zach waited for the dented convertible to appear in the driveway and for Carhart, his heavy shoes clanging on the steel steps, to climb the outside stairs to his third-floor apartment.

Carhart's appearance set his teeth on edge. When Carhart turned the light on in his double window, Zach used his binoculars to spy, hoping to catch a glimpse of the big blowhard wearing a farmer's straw hat, sitting in his bathtub and strumming a guitar. Sometimes the insurance salesman had a shot glass of whiskey at his elbow and a corncob pipe clenched in his teeth. The whiskey made Zach thirsty, but the black smoke that coiled against the wall and draped around Tony's dented straw brim seemed ominous to Zach. He watched Tony Carhart strum the guitar and mouth song lyrics while he leaned his head back to gaze out the window at the silver, featureless moon hanging in the sky with the blank, imperturbable face that resembled his own.

Last March, there had been a knock at the door. Zach had discovered a stranger standing in the hallway, leaning one spidery arm against the door frame, holding a battered leather briefcase in the other. He had on an old-fashioned fedora hat and camel-hair topcoat; a shiny silk tie peeked under his collar, and his pointed-toe shoes were polished to a high gloss. "Hello, neighbor," the stranger had said. The stranger was Carhart. He introduced himself and flashed an identity card. "This is your lucky day. I work for the Epic Life Insurance Company of America and I'm here to protect your future."

"This ain't my lucky day," Zach said, blocking the doorway.

Tony Carhart showed straight polished teeth and offered a wolfish smile. "You appear to be someone who could use some sound financial advice," he said.

"Nobody ever talks to me. People think I'm crazy," Zach said.

"I don't give a damn what people think, son."

"I ain't nobody's son. I'm an orphan."

"As long as you have the money to pay Epic's low-cost insurance premiums, you're all right with me," Tony Carhart said.

"I get my money from the government but I don't need no insurance cost since I don't have no one to care for if I'm dead."

"I like a young man with a practical attitude, but have you thought of the cost of your burial?" Tony Carhart intoned in his smooth baritone voice. "You don't want to be buried in an unmarked grave in some Potters Field. Or worse, die in the street and get e't by crows, which happened to a man in Schenectady, New York just last year. I got an article in my wallet that says the crows picked his bones clean except for his elastic bowtie and his empty wallet. You want to see it?" He reached for his wallet but Zach held up his hands to stop him.

"It won't matter where I'm buried. I won't be around to see it. Sure, I got a plot but they could burn my bones for all I care, and I don't have a wallet," Zach said.

"A smart fella like you needs to prepare for the future. Ain't you thinking of marrying?"

"You tell me when the future begins and I'll start preparing for it then."

On Saturday nights Zach watched Carhart with increasing jealousy, as he escorted Holly Belcamp to his apartment. Using the binoculars, Zach observed every detail of their shadows dancing on the window shade. He watched them until the lights went out and then he continued to stare into the dark. He kept count of the times Holly stayed overnight. He thought the number might be fifteen. He watched for months.

Zach spied on all of Carhart's women, alerted to their comings and goings by their shoes clanking on the outdoor stairs leading to the third-floor apartment. He watched a tall woman with taffy-colored curls. When she threw open the window and sang opera, she woke the neighborhood. Her antics made Zach want to laugh out loud—he stuffed his mouth with his fist so as not to be heard. Next evening, he watched a short blonde woman shaped like a tea kettle pull the shade off its rollers when she entered the room, and Carhart in his shirtsleeves climb a stepladder to replace the shade with a bedsheet he tacked to the window frame with a staple gun. But the most curious behavior was when Carhart escorted an older gray-haired woman who wobbled in her flat shoes as she traversed the steep stairs. He noted the insurance man always opened the car door for her. If she shivered, he wrapped her in his topcoat. When they climbed the three flights of stairs to his apartment, he even lent the woman his shoulder to lean on, and once, in a rainstorm, he spread his slicker across a puddle, allowing her to step off the sidewalk without wetting her feet. Zach reasoned that Carhart fussed over the older woman because she was his mother.

But Zach paid the most attention to Holly Belcamp. One day soon he would talk to her, but when he met her on the sidewalk heading home in the evening, she crossed the street or ducked into a store. To counter this, Zach learned Holly's schedule, and waited just beyond her front steps. He hoped to catch her before she had time to avoid him, but when she appeared, balancing a grocery bag in one arm, she brushed by him with her chin raised as if he were no more than a bug skittering across the concrete.

In his weekly therapy sessions with Doctor Marjorie May, Zach never mentioned Carhart or Carhart's mother. Mostly he talked of not being able to sleep. Dr. Marjorie prescribed his medication, as well as a powdered doughnut with warm chocolate milk before bedtime as a sleep aid. She recommended breathing exercises to manage his anxiety. She smiled approvingly when Zach shared his thoughts about Holly. Realizing Doctor Marjorie was as interested in Holly Belcamp as he was, Zach began to fill his sessions with talk about Holly. Doctor Marjorie was a tall, slender woman with a single braid of iron-gray hair. Sitting in a big recliner while gazing out the bay window onto the hospital's flowerbeds and lawns, she crossed her skinny legs under a long plaid skirt and wrote her notes in a grade-school composition book. She was a person of few words but when she spoke, she looked him dead in the eye and her gaze was piercing. Then Zach felt like a moth under glass in the Sylvia Hardwell Dix Natural History Museum, where he worked as a security guard. He squirmed in his chair to free himself of the trapped feeling—an exercise Dr. Marjorie encouraged. Soon, in every session, he detailed Holly's comings and goings in what Dr. Marjorie called a "debriefing." He practiced interrogation evasion—he didn't reveal that he watched Holly from his window. Without ever saying it, he implied that Holly and he were friends. When he finally did give his secret away, Dr. Marjorie looked pleased. She asked questions about the binoculars, and suggested he might one day introduce himself as a neighbor.

Another thing changed in Zach's life. Instead of the highway, he began walking on Dix Hollow's tree-lined streets, looking into people's windows to observe how they lived. He preferred the populated neighborhoods to prowling the dark woods beside the highway. Dr. Marjorie saw this as progress, since Zach had grown up in Dix Hollow. In those days, when the town abutted the hospital grounds, the town had been merely two streets of store fronts, a covered train platform, and the orange GLF warehouse with its wooden weathervane crudely carved to resemble an ear of corn. Now, the area had spread into miles of winding, tree-lined streets of split-level and Cape Cod homes, paved driveways, trimmed shrubs, and immaculate lawns. Every driveway had at least one shiny new automobile, and the downtown had become a hodgepodge of strip malls. The diner Zach had once eaten at with his high school friends had been bought by a Chinese takeout restaurant. A tanning salon had taken over the hardware store. The bowling alley had been replaced by a dance studio. But Zach remembered the town as it once was. He liked walking the streets in every direction and remembering, and he soon discovered that by dusk, when the house lights were on, he could see through the big front windows into living rooms where husbands and wives often sat with their children watching shows on their enormous TV sets while eating their supper from cardboard trays.

On Saturday and Sunday mornings, Zach woke before dawn to mop and wax the museum's terracotta and marble floors. He had been given the job by Doc Shaw, who claimed to have once spent a week recuperating from exhaustion in the nearby hospital. The clasp knife Zach carried in his trouser pocket had once belonged to Doc Shaw, who wasn't actually a doctor, but a retired O.T., and although Zach never found out the man's first name, he always liked him and was pleased when "Old Shaw," as he called himself, had given him the knife. "In case yah have to jimmy a lock on an exhibit case or pry open a stuck window… Just don't slice off yah thumb," the old man had warned. Doc Shaw taught him to operate an electric buffing machine, sweeping the machine side to side across the floor. The buffer resembled a small flying saucer attached to a broom handle, and Zach learned to work the machine with an easy sweeping motion. The heavy exercise made his forearms bulge.

The museum had lifelike exhibits displayed in domed glass cabinets, and once a month, besides polishing the floors and guarding the exhibits, Zach polished the glass cabinets. One of those mornings when Zach polished the glass, he saw Tony Carhart entering the museum with a new woman. Pretending to tie his laces, Zach ducked behind a concrete urn. The woman had on a flower print scarf that hid her hair, a long plaid skirt, and a bright purple sweater. Zach swallowed hard. He felt his cheeks get hot. When the woman turned toward him, he saw she had on bright pink lipstick that matched her sweater. He thought she might be Dr. Marjorie May. He rubbed his eyes and looked again, and from a distance, followed the pair as they toured the displays, only to discover, as the woman removed her head scarf to drink at a water fountain, that he was not looking at Dr. Marjorie after all, but a much younger woman with golden hair.

Every Saturday and Sunday, Zach took up his post beside the large concrete urn in the Great Zoology Hall that had three stuffed, indigenous species of deer in a large, glass-domed display. A red-tailed hawk hung from a wire circling over a sky painted pale blue. A forest of tall pines made of papier-mâché shimmered in the flood lights. On the forest floor, made of ceramic clay, a snarling red fox hid in red-stenciled paper ivy, and a fat badger with tiny, ink-black eyes made of glass peered out of a cardboard log. All day, visitors asked questions about the diorama—he rarely knew the answers, so he made things up, telling them that badgers made sounds like canaries, or that red-tailed hawks liked eating peanuts. Sometimes, a child tried to climb under the rope line into the display. Then Zach had to pull back the kicking and screaming child and deliver him head-first into the arms of the horror-stricken parents, whose dismayed frowns often silently accused Zach of being insensitive and rough. He had to admit he knew nothing about children, but he had to enforce the rule that forbid museum visitors to cross the rope.

The one Saturday when Holly Belcamp toured the museum, Zach stood stiffly in the center of the Great Zoology Hall with his hands clasped behind his back and his chin tucked in. He stood in the center of the room to make certain she saw him. He regretted his uniform wasn't freshly pressed, and the more he thought about the uniform hanging off his body, limp and damp, the more rumpled and creased the uniform seemed. He called out Holly's name, but she had moved on to the next exhibit.

But he did catch her eye for a moment, and for a long time after, he could recall the deep brown shade of her irises, and he saw, or thought he saw, one eyebrow flicker in an amused way and something like a lush smile skip across her mouth. She held a pamphlet in one hand, a small prim purse in the other. She had on what he called a slinky skirt, black stockings, tall shiny boots and a short, form-fitting coat that showed her figure. He thought she sighed when he said hello, though he wasn't even certain he had spoken. Then she passed down the hallway and he stood, noting with some satisfaction, that she had come to the museum by herself. But he had not introduced himself or warned her of Tony Carhart. Perhaps he had not said anything at all.

Dr. Marjorie encouraged Zach to make friends. "There are so many people living by themselves," she said and offered him a glossy pamphlet. Zach glanced over the pamphlet of adult learning courses given by the community college while Dr. Marjorie leaned back in her leather reclining chair and waited. Besides the numerous vocational courses, such as "Introduction to Heating, Ventilation, and Air Conditioning," and "Computer Programming Made Simple," there was a Chinese cooking course, which Zach ruled out because he did all his cooking on a hot plate; a course in "Defensive Driving" that seemed pointless, as Zach was legally forbidden to drive; and a course named "A Traveler's Guide to Europe" that Zach discounted since he didn't have money to travel.

When Zach placed the pamphlet on his chair without making a choice, Dr. Marjorie frowned. "You have to do something," she said in an exasperated voice. "Spending all your time alone isn't going to help you get well."

"I'm not sick," Zach said. "I just like keeping to myself."

"It isn't healthy," Dr. Marjorie said. "You'll shrivel up."

"I want to spend my time with Holly."

"Well then, go up to her and introduce yourself. Tell her you're new in town."

"I can't say that. I've lived here all my life."

"Well, come up with something," Dr. Marjorie said. "You don't want to be alone forever."

One day, Tony Carhart discovered Zach waiting on the street beside Holly Belcamp's mailbox. Tony came right up to him, swinging his briefcase and glowering. Before Zach could explain he was there for his government check, Tony said, "Stop following Holly!" Zack felt the impulse to throw a punch, but not wanting another stay in the hospital, he controlled his temper and drew long, deep breaths as Dr. Marjorie had taught him.

"It's a free country," he answered.

"You keep following her and it won't be free for you," Tony Carhart said.

"I just want to meet her," Zach said.

"Then act like a normal person."

With his jaw clamped tight, Zach stood there, unable to explain himself. He continued his breathing exercises until he was calm enough to cross the street.

He watched Carhart laboring to climb the outdoor stairs and enter his third-floor apartment. Time seemed to hover in the air like fragments of a geometrical pattern. Later, when the postman came lumbering down the sidewalk carrying his mailbag over his shoulder, Zach went to pick his envelope from the bag, but the postman stopped him. "What the hell do you think you're doing?" he hollered. Then he made Zach stand aside, and with a show of officious self-importance, the postman thumbed through every single piece of mail before handing Zach the one envelope addressed to him. Zach tore the envelope open and held the green government check between his thumb and forefinger like a captured butterfly.

In spite of Tony Carhart's warning, most evenings Zach waited behind the front hedge for the lovely Holly. Sometimes Holly didn't show up, and sometimes she came late, long after Zach had left his post to eat a canned spaghetti supper in his room. Then, after ten days waiting, he met her at her door. Though he stammered, he managed to say, "I've seen you at the Sylvia Hardwell Dix Natural History Museum in the Great Zoological Hall… I had just waxed the floor."

Holly Belcamp stared—her brown eyes wide, brows raised, mouth set in a plucky smile meant to conceal surprise. "That's nice," she said.

"My name's Zach," he said. "I live on the street."

"Sorry, Zach, I don't have spare change."

"I'm not homeless," he said. "I rent a room in the house across the street from you."

He pointed to the house in the general vicinity of the room that faced her window.

"Oh," she said. "You mean we live on the same street."

"Yes, we do."

"That's sweet, Zach. You'll excuse me. I have to be going."

Zach stepped forward. Quickly enveloped by the scent of her powder and lipstick, and by her white-blonde hair the color of lightning, he warned her of Tony Carhart's treachery and leaned so close to her face he saw tiny purple veins in the whites of her eyes. He saw little red creases in the corners of her mouth as she whispered hello.

Then she was gone and he saw garbled geometrical patterns like fireflies swarming in the forest, flashing before his eyes. He tumbled through the swarm, down through the tree branches, floating side to side like a leaf swaying in the wind. He smacked the forest floor with his chin. He saw a fountain of sparks. He felt the bump. His chin was wet—it was blood dripping onto his clothes.

"I never got your phone number," Zach shouted into the darkness.

He waited at his window until the moon came floating over the houses. The yellowish three-quarter moon cast an excess of dull golden light on the peaked roofs and bare outstretched trees as it rode up on the pale winter sky. In his room, the illuminated numbers on his broken digital clock kept flashing 14:58. He went downstairs and tiptoed out the back entrance, making certain the door didn't slam and disturb the other boarders, who might complain. He already noticed them giving him wary looks when he ran into them on the stairs. He crossed the yard, ducking behind the bushes, telling himself he would use Doc Shaw's knife for a purpose. He imagined himself a hunter but he did not let himself think of what his prey might be. He climbed the steel stairs of the apartment house, and then, hugging the drainpipe with his arms, he used his legs to shimmy the pipe until he could pull himself over the rain gutter, onto the roof. Flat on his belly, the rough texture of shingles scraping his cheek, he hunkered down to wait, surveying the neighborhood houses, observing the warm lights in their windows and the families moving about inside—eating, talking, watching TV—doing the ordinary things people do together, the ordinary things in life that excluded him.

A dog barked in some yard, the animal's lonely woofing reminding Zach of his own longings. Then he imagined each house had a personality, like the people who lived in them. The house where Holly Belcamp resided, with its scrolled cornices and wraparound porch, had a stately reserve. The house where Tony Carhart brought his girlfriends and his mother had a stubby chimney and narrow front steps surrounded by ragged forsythia bushes. Weather-beaten shutters hung off its windows. Carhart's house felt crude. Even the boarding house where Zach lived had a personality. It had a rutted driveway, a splintered porch railing, windows hung with different coverings—a print curtain, a gray window shade, a set of heavy wooden blinds. Its disjointed façade was like a confused person wearing used, mismatched clothes.

He rolled onto his back and observed the winter night. An ocean of stars stretched across the sky, an infinite radiance he wanted to name, but he was suddenly distracted by a car's double beam headlights shining in the driveway below. He lifted himself down from the roof, over the railing, and onto the steel platform supporting the stairs. Below him, Tony Carhart's heavy shoes struck loudly on the steel steps. Carhart staggered as if he might be drunk. Zach descended. Even in the dark, he could see the outline of Carhart's broad muscular shoulders, his round head and shining blond hair streaked with moonlight, the folds in Carhart's thick neck and his fleshy ears glinting like pieces of chrome. Zach stepped lightly on the rungs so that his rubber-soled sneakers made no sound except for a drumming vibration he felt in his toes.

Tony Carhart waited at the foot of the stairs. But there was something about Tony Carhart standing there, even with his arrogant chin and his tan wool suit, his expensive topcoat cinched at the waist with the broad collar turned out the way Hollywood stars wore them, that told Zach this had been a bad night for Tony. He had red-rimmed eyes, his hawk nose was reddened at the tip, and his tousled blond pompadour resembled a haystack blown down by the wind.

Zach felt around his pocket for Doc Shaw's old knife. The crosshatched grips were cold in his palm. When he showed Tony Carhart a friendly grin, he thought of the grin Doc Shaw had shown the snooty visitors at the museum. Tony replied with a quick nod. He was unsteady on the steps. Then Zach heard the older woman sigh, saw her stumble, and with both hands grab at the railing, then pitch forward headfirst. Zach broke her fall by reaching over the bannister to catch her by the ankles so that she slid slowly, like a heavy package on skids, down the steps with her loose shoes slapping her bare heels like a pair of floppy slippers, her hair dragging after her. He just caught hold of a thick ankle before she rolled onto the sidewalk, and while grappling with her ankle, he looked her in the face. She was a bit younger than he thought. She had a wide-eyed surprised look, her painted mouth half-open as if she had been stopped in mid-sentence by some rude interruption. Her complexion reminded him of the gray grit of the desert in the museum's southwest exhibit. He put his ear to her chest and listened. Beside her, an open pocketbook lay on its side; cosmetics and keys and other small items scattered around were glinting in the light from the street lamp. The woman's heart was not beating.

Then Tony Carhart knelt down. "I called for help," he whispered to the woman, "they'll be coming soon."

Zach said, "But she could sure use a blanket!"

Breath steamed from Tony's nostrils and the heavy odor of his sickly-sweet cologne made Zach so nauseous his palms began to sweat. He bit his tongue in a struggle to hold himself together in front of another human being. Tony must have guessed his condition and he grumbled in his arrogant way, showing his big front teeth. "You sure you know what the hell you're doing?" he croaked.

"She needs a blanket," Zach answered, his voice quavering. "Or she'll go into shock." It was all he could think to say.

"Okay, use my coat," Carhart responded in an irritable tone.

Zach reached for the expensive, camel-hair coat with big leather buttons and leather collar and he guessed it was warm. He spread the coat over the woman and then knelt to begin CPR, something he remembered from long ago, when he had been someone, before the disease had overtaken him, sometimes rendering his thoughts in a dizzy cavalcade. Back then, when he had a name and a shape, he had known himself; that is, he had seen enough to know where he ended and where the world began. CPR had been his first aid training for the town's volunteer ambulance corps, which he never joined. He remembered the shiny red and white ambulance with its chrome siren and flashing lights on the roof, and the dozen volunteer members, whose names he had forgotten, in their khaki uniforms, silver name tags pinned to their pocket flaps, posing for a photograph outside the ambulance corps garage while he watched, hidden in a strip of nearby woods. He saw their easy grins and the confidence he lacked exuding from their faces. Then he shut his eyes and exhaled breath into the old woman's mouth, pushed and pounded and put his ear to her chest and listened, and when her heartbeat came back, it sounded something like fingers drumming a rubber band. He jumped in the air and whooped before he caught himself, and remembering the ambulance corps protocol, he put on a serious face and knelt over the woman to watch her in his detached way, while Tony, holding his phone to his ear, shouted at the emergency operator. Had he done all he could? He was reassured when the woman's eyes flickered open. She was trying to say something. Her mouth moved, and Zach, listening to her pulse, saw what he imagined as the glint of life in her eyes. Or it might have been moonlight—he couldn't be sure. When she tried to speak, he watched her crumpled lips. He saw her struggle for words. What was she trying to say?

"You're going to be alright," he said.

"Where's the damn EMS?" Tony said, shivering and shouting as if it were Zach's miscalculation that delayed them.

"You're going to be alright," Zach said to the woman. "Stay with me."

"I hear the siren, Lillian. They're coming," Tony said, peering over Zach's shoulder.

"Help…" the woman coughed in a raspy whisper.

But Zach had done all he could.

"Stay with me," he repeated. "Stay with me." He stared into the trickle of light in Lillian's watery gray eyes while he listened to the ambulance siren—a long, terrifying scream that seemed to come from inside his head. He could do nothing but reassure this woman, and Carhart, who could not even do that, muttered over Zach's shoulder in a furious way, spluttering and spitting, interfering with Zach's every effort to calm the woman. In spite of Carhart's meddling, Zach managed to encourage her to breathe rhythmically the way Doctor Marjorie had taught him to. He rolled his jacket into a ball and used it to elevate her feet so blood would flow to her head to prevent her from going into shock. He talked gently and rubbed the woman's wrists, and when she turned her pale head to mumble gratefully at Carhart, but never looked at Zach, Zach felt relief that she was conscious, and rage at being ignored. He told himself she was just another stranger. It shouldn't matter she hadn't noticed his efforts. The woman was merely a stranger and shouldn't matter to him at all, even if he had saved her life—even if he felt he knew her in some deeper way that he couldn't explain to himself or anyone.

Tony Carhart's habitually smug expression had returned and he seemed peeved that Zach had taken charge in the emergency. His face had an odd look. His eyes were slits, his mouth tilted to one side, his beak nose white as bone. Carhart's face reminded Zach of a death mask from the museum's Pacific Island exhibit. Zach turned away to banish the image from his mind. But he continued to visualize the death masks and shrunken heads from the exhibit. He kept going over the grateful expression the stricken woman had shown to Carhart. Then, from the habit of putting his bad thoughts out of his mind, he watched Holly Belcamp's nighttime window. Gazing at Holly's window had always been his escape; this time, though, he didn't actually look inside until he saw Holly's light go on and Holly lean over the sill to stare into the driveway. Had the lovely Holly actually seen him spring into action? He saw or thought he saw her face show distress, concern, or approval. But she quickly withdrew behind the curtains and the window went dark.

She was lost to him again, another casualty of his mind, and Zach experienced the same helpless feeling he always felt. But this time, he would have a witness, because the woman on the sidewalk would live. He felt his stomach aching, a sour taste rising, mixing with a wave of happiness. A happiness that he supposed would last forever. Then his head spun with bright lights as if all the stars had begun to dart around him like fireflies.

This Poem Is About a Folk Song

Andie Francis

The song is about a train
called the midnight special,
brother. The lights on the train
are bright. The only wind
comes from its barreling.
Let's gather everything
we've bartered. The smokes,
neat in their boxes. We'll load up
our pockets and bicker. No, you
ate the honey buns. Let's see
before the train's big haul.
I'll stand on your shoulders,
give me a boost. How much
do you know about this world
when things can't just be?
When a piece of paper
is enough to make you go blind?
Let her apron alone, let her
cry out back. Our troubles
are lousy birthmarks.

Brother, I've found
the everlasting light in this
breeze. Let it shine us bare.

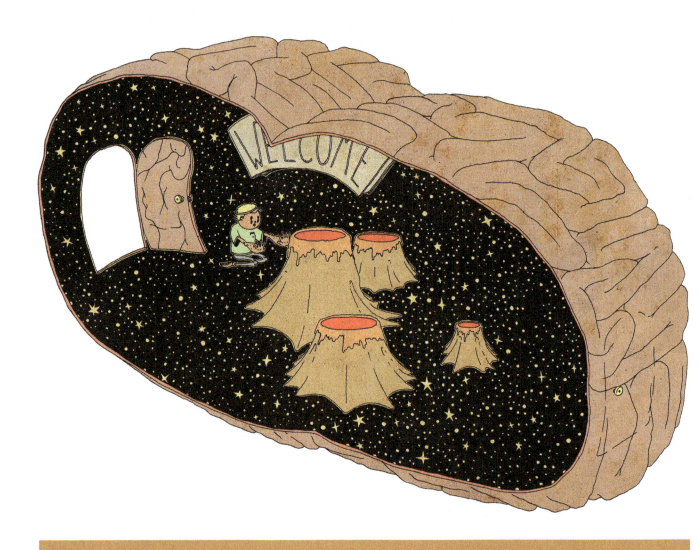

"Untitled" by George Davis Cathcart

Thief of Holes

Mark Crimmins

Go to the doughnut shop. Buy six doughnut holes for ninety-nine cents. Eat the doughnut holes with satisfaction because you are doing something impossible. You are eating holes! Get into the habit of going to the doughnut shop and buying six doughnut holes every afternoon on your break during shifts at the library. Get to liking these doughnut holes. Say to yourself in your mind around three o'clock every affee: *Gettin ready for mah holes*! Imagine someone stopping you and asking what you have in the bag. Imagine yourself replying, *Uh, just a bunch of holes*. Like America for inventing an edible hole. Think: in England they wouldn't have allowed them to be called doughnut holes precisely because it doesn't make sense to buy a hole. Think: in England they would have had to call them something else. Doughnut balls. Doughnut centres. Doughnut middles. Go every day to the doughnut shop and buy six doughnut holes for ninety-nine cents. Like America for having so many ninety-nine cent food deals. Four tacos from

Taco Time. Four plain burgers from Dee's. Wendy's all-you-can-eat French toast between 6.00 and 7.00 a.m. Six doughnut holes for ninety-nine cents. Go to the doughnut shop. Buy six doughnut holes for ninety-nine cents. Eat the doughnut holes with satisfaction because you are doing something impossible. Eating a bag full of holes! Become addicted to doughnut holes. Make up little songs about doughnut holes. Theorize doughnut holes as *absent centres*. Notice the student worker with the funky blue hair at the doughnut shop on campus does not really count the holes in your bag when you buy them at her register. Buy six doughnut holes for ninety-nine cents. Eat the doughnut holes with satisfaction because you are engaging in an oxymoronic act. Eating a hole! Make up little advertising jingles for the doughnut company. *I'm not crazy about doughnuts but I'm a sucker for holes! I needed to lose a little weight so I just started nibbling holes!* Notice the girl again. Miss I-Don't-Give-A-Shit-About-This-Job Blue Hair. Observe that she doesn't deign to look into the bag. Just rings it up. Become addicted to holes. Build up a tolerance to holes so that six isn't enough. Watch Blue Hair closely. Always pick her line. See yourself in front of a judge making a speech. *Your Honor, I just felt—probably incorrectly—that it was sort of impossible to steal a hole.* Go to the doughnut shop. Slip a seventh doughnut hole in the bag. Take it to Blue Hair. Say, very casually, *Uh, I got the six-doughnut-hole deal.* Smile when she says, *Yeah, I think I figured that one out.* Resist the temptation to fraternize with Blue Hair. Keep that professional distance. Get seven doughnut holes for ninety-nine cents! As you bite into the seventh doughnut hole, the stolen hole, remember a Biblical proverb. *Bread eaten in secret is pleasant.* Go to the doughnut shop. Buy seven doughnut holes for ninety-nine cents. Go to the doughnut shop. Buy eight doughnut holes for ninety-nine cents. Go to the doughnut shop. Buy nine doughnut holes for ninety-nine cents! Love Blue Hair! Love America! Go to the doughnut shop. Go to the doughnut shop. Just to mix it up, once in a while actually buy six doughnut holes for ninety-nine cents. Keep a little register listing all the doughnut holes you have stolen. Note the flavor of the stolen holes. Reflect on the dominance of the chocolate cocoanut hole. Make a goal to steal a thousand doughnut holes overall. Get ambitious on your own ass. Go to the doughnut shop. Buy ten doughnut holes, eleven doughnut holes, twelve doughnut holes for ninety-nine cents! Imagine the doughnut shop going out of business and not being able to figure out where all the money went. Wonder how high you can go. Picture yourself pushing a wheelbarrow overflowing with hundreds of doughnut holes up to Blue Hair's register and brazenly announcing, *Six doughnut holes!* Make Blue Hair into an idol that you worship in a little shrine. Pray to Blue Hair. Patron Saint of Doughnut Holes. Translate 'doughnut holes' into Mexican Spanish. *Agujeros de donas.* Think of Blue Hair as *Nuestra Señora de Agujeros de Donas.* Try to envision the upper limit of your fraudulence. See it as determined by the parameters of the doughnut bag. Go to the doughnut shop. Worry about the bad luck of buying thirteen doughnut holes for ninety-nine cents. Think uncomfortably that the overflowing bag on the counter in front of Blue Hair looks like a tiny sack of potatoes. Eat the doughnut holes with satisfaction because you are eating an impossibility. A bunch of stolen holes! Start to get a bit queasy from how many doughnut holes you are eating. Tell your girlfriend it must be stress when she says you seem to be putting on weight. Sail over the edge of buying thirteen doughnut holes for ninety-nine cents. Keep writing in your leger with columns and numbers and flavors. Start writing things down in ciphers in case the campus police nail you. *Cops Arrest Doughnut Hole Thief.* See yourself in a camp outfit that includes a sombrero. Invent a name for yourself. *The Mad Doughnut Hole Eater.* Hear little kids whining to their parents about getting a Mad Doughnut Hole Eater Doll as a birthday present. Start probing the upper limits of what the little doughnut bag can hold. Go to the doughnut shop. Buy fifteen doughnut holes for ninety-nine cents! Buy sixteen doughnut holes for ninety-nine cents! Finally, stuff an incredible seventeen doughnut holes into the bursting bag and pay Blue Hair ninety-nine cents for six! Have an epiphany. Quit while you're ahead. Stop there and go back to six. Declare an end to your life of crime. Give it up. Reform. Lose yourself in the rediscovered pleasure of six.

Chowder: *Moby Dick* Chapter 15

Jessica Cuello

Leave the iron down with me.

Housekeeping and sexless,
I find the unmade bed, the tooth left.
I do not stop to feel. I feed the men.
Chop clams. Think I don't know
I'm the laugh and lackey?
Think I don't—

I carry bowls, I nag, begin. Alone
I undress my body—this dark home—
heavy, fish-smelling.
I set my necklace of polished
fish vertebrae on the dresser
and remember Mother's dry
arthritic hands that served
when they couldn't bend.

Leave the iron down with me.

I'm stopping death.
I found a body pierced

with a harpoon—an accident.
I'm making soup.
Thankless stirring,
the leftover of woman.

"Untitled" by George Davis Cathcart

A Friend of the World

Nathan Leslie

People make things more complicated than necessary. They're simple. Rule #27—you try hard, you succeed. I buy it. I work it. I stay laser-like, and I'm golden. I stray, lose myself in what so-and-so is wearing or look up—big trouble. Cameras.

Rule #14—just follow through. Which Chief says means do as you're told. Which means take the order and process it. Like a cook in a restaurant. I wouldn't be caught dead.

I'm good. I believe that. Mr. Lannon says I'm "disciplined." Says it's a rare trait to have. I'm studying criminology. For a reason. Other reasons too, but the main reason is I want to be a detective. Always liked the idea of tracking, hunting, figuring out the puzzle. That's the challenge—putting it all together.

The girl who sits next to me is always in her pocket texting her boys. Knuckles pumping fabric. By "boys" I mean friends, not boyfriends. So she says. What do I know? She's smoking. It's in the eyes—pupils big as quarters, Caribbean blue. I'm a sucker for a pretty face. The rest don't even matter to me. When the face is pretty, the rest follows. And she's popping.

A nice smile is all I need.

We're in the Sporting Goods Store. Chief says he wants the RG2s. All sizes. Tough because shoes are big, bulky. Ally is on watchdog, so she's eyeballing. We're in the shadow by the pillar. Electronic eyes can't go there. We've hit them before. Many times.

I'm snapping the alligator tags behind the pillar. It's like plastic crab legs. I got a dozen that one time. The sun. The wind. The pinging docks.

I get three pair into my booster bag and three more in Ally's. Home Depot—since there's one adjacent. They think we must have a bunch of hammers and nails or some shit on top of the lining. We've got layers of sandpaper, paint brushes and paint samples. So there you go.

Ally's a good sight. No snooping clerks or assistant managers say shit. We buy a can of racquetballs. Cashier says, "You find everything okay?"

"I think so, honey," I say. "Didn't we?"

"Yes, dear," ally says. She's sucking on a Lifesaver, smacking her lips.

"You know, we forgot the primer," I say. Bullshit small talk is the best distractor. Chief taught us well.

"Oh, we did," Ally says, almost sarcastic.

The cashier drops the can of racquetballs in the bag, then the receipt.

What does he care? We could lift a kayak, and as long as he doesn't get reprimanded he's solid. Big Polynesian-looking guy with a wide face and gold earring in his right ear. Gives him the look of Mr. Clean, just a bit.

Me and Ally walk out slow, holding hands. This is the only part that gives me cramps. The detector. Chief says just to turn around and shrug shoulders. Cashiers are used to falsies and (again) don't really care anyway. The percents are in our favor, he says. But it doesn't happen. We walk right through, bags in the trunk and drive away. Nine hundred worth of shoes, cleancleanclean.

I imagine Ally clothesless. I don't have to. I don't exactly want her, so it goes. But still. You work with someone enough, you can get used to the idea. There are worse things to adjust to. Plus, she knows this side of me. Nobody else does, except the others Chief brought in. And Chief, of course.

He shows nothing when we drop the shoes off at the port. No smile. No thank you. This is how he does it. Keeps us craving for approval. Just a little acknowledgement, something.

We line them up on the fold-out. It's all kinds of stuff. Watches, DVDs, deodorant, medications, knives, smart phones, lamps, clocks, soap, batteries, books, coffee, detergent. Everything jumbled together, no order. He shows nothing, gives nothing.

"I'll call you soon," he says. That "soon" is promising. That's about as close to a "good job" as I've received.

Don't let him down, though. He'll tear you up.

Chief looks like an African warlord. And he's African. Rumor has it, Cameroon. But others say Niger. He's not a nice man. He's not your friend. It's all business all the time. Money runs through his veins.

It's fine with me. Less complicated this way.

The fluorescents buzz and moths ping against them. It smells like cat piss in there. Always does, always will.

"Hey, Mom," I say. "Home."

She kisses my cheeks, says she couldn't wait until I come home. She spoils me like a grandmother would. I'm the youngest, so that could have something to do with it.

"I got you something," she says. As if today is different from any other. She's always giving me something.

She hands me a box. Says, Open it. It's RX2s, running shoes. I about crap myself, thinking she must know. Thinking it's a sign. Thinking it's a subtle hint she's trying to send me. But when I watch her face I don't see that in her. She's just trying to encourage me. Track, which is what I'm best at in life. Pure speed. When I'm working for Chief I always know I can outrun any rent-a cop who might try to chase me down.

I'm hunting a cheetah. I close my eyes and I'm flying through the grass and the sun is warm against the back of my neck and I'm gaining on him. No human has run so fast before. I've got my RX2s and my mother is by the tree watching me fly, clapping her hands. I can hear her and the pounding of the cheetah as I gain on him. I can smell his tart sweat and the katydids in the grasses leap up as we run. Some thwack against my face. And.

"Do you like them?"

"Thanks, Mom. Yeah."

It's possible she's making up for everything before. Her guilt is an engine. It's okay, though. I'll take it.

"That shit was tight," Ally says.

"I know, right?"

"It was like we were invisible. They didn't even see us."

"I know."

Chief glowers. We're sitting there in the back. The buzz is going from the fluorescents. Chief is drinking Red Bull and vodka, spitting sunflower seeds on the floor. Nobody is talking.

Chief just gave a speech about how we needed to "up the ante." More supply needed. We're constantly running out of product, he said. Who wouldn't want two gallons of Tide for five bucks? At the store it would be four times that.

"We're doing the people a service," he said. "You remember Robin the Hood, right? This shit is our Nottinghood Forest."

I didn't want to say anything.

Ally calls him Neg Nan (Negative Nancy).

Ally and me are in the Gucci Giant—bigbigbig. This get is totally different. There are people everywhere. It's not like you can just slip anything in your pocket without looking. The razor blades and condoms are all behind glass anyway.

Chief wants Tide. If not Tide then Downy. If not Downy then the generic.

Ally has the shopping cart parked in the detergent aisle and I'm dropping two-gallon bottles in there, as many as we can squeeze in. Lady passes us, giving us a dirty look. Stringy lady with a rooster head. She looks back at us as if she knows. I think she might say something. But she doesn't.

The cart is heavy as shit. Ally can't push it. This isn't a good start, I think.

"We both need to do it," I say.

Our car is parked around back.

"It's too heavy," she says.

So we're pushing it toward the door, but dropping ballast as we go. Too much, too much. Three less and it feels as if we can go fast, which is what we want.

We pull up to the bulletin board next to the exit. No detector at all. I glance back and don't see anybody eyeballing. Could be a renta up in the ceiling on the cams. But I doubt it. Not at a grocery store.

I slowly nose it in the right direction. Ally sidles next to me.

I whisper. "One. Two. Three."

We push as fast as we can right out the automatic. We're flying past the old ladies on the sidewalk, nearly knock over a girl collecting donations. I've never pushed so fast in my life. Those new treads Moms hit me with work like a charm.

"Wait," I hear behind us. I don't stop to find out.

We turn the corner, race down the sidewalk. Ally pops the doors. We are hurling the detergent in, two at a time. Someone is yelling. She hops around and in. I slide in back. A cashier is churning after us, outfit flailing. But it's too late—we crash the cart and peel out of there.

We're laughing. We get a few miles off, duck onto a side street. At the light I kiss her. My tongue inside her tongue. She flushes and smacks the steering wheel. We turn up the ska. It's all she listens to and I'm happy to go along. I pound along on the dashboard.

Mr. Gannon is talking about borderline cases. He says if law was out and dry it wouldn't change. He says law is dynamic and enforcement of it is constantly evolving, changing, mutating. He says it's like an organism.

He brings up the example of student cheating.

"We all know plagiarism is wrong, but is it 'illegal,' per se? Not really. You can't be *arrested* for plagiarism. You can't even be arrested for being one of those guys who runs the plagiarizing websites. You can help hundreds of students all over America cheat and you're safe. Is that right?"

"No," I say. "If it was, it wouldn't feel wrong? Not that I know from experience."

Laughing.

"A feel, good. Interesting point about the role of intuition. Has anyone done something wrong that they later feel guilty about?"

I don't say anything.

I wish Ally was here. She's harder than me, more able to shoot down ideas she doesn't like.

Nobody says anything. Tough question to get a response to.

Borderline. Who isn't on some kind of border or another?

Chief hands one an extra ten.

"Good," he says. He means the Tide.

I nod. This is a loud thank you for him. I exhale. Praise accepted.

"It's hard," he says. "Grocery, very tough."

I nod. It's a great day.

I never heard back from Ally. She doesn't text me. Nothing.

It's Jess and Felix and Paul and me. We're eating candy corn even though its spring. Felix found them in the back. They taste sour or something, and I'm wondering if candy corn can go bad.

He has the others hit another grocery, different part of town. He says I've earned my solo.

"You know what 'lollygag' means?"

"No," I say.

"Go casual." He means the mall.

"Lollygag" means a "friendly." Not friendly like I'm out to make friends. Have to be smart, not take anything easy. It means I pick what I want. This takes the pressure off.

I don't like the mall. Too many kids my age I might bump into, too much sex in the eye. I walk past Victoria's Secret. All that cleavage and fuck-me stares—too much. Easier going to the family stores. I remember there used to be an arcade on one of the side corridors. Gone now—everything has its time. I duck into the religious bookstore—only one in the mall. I'm leafing through books telling me how to follow Jesus, how to live saintly, how to eat Christian, how to feel right about the world. The nice leather Bibles are up front. I never knew so many different kinds. The Bibles are popping. Brown Bibles. Red Bibles. Black bibles. I like the black Bible with the gold cross. It looks like the kind you could swear an oath on, for real. Something the Pope might carry.

There's no detector, so I carry it to my side down the back. It's just one orange-haired black lady with a nice smile, me, and a couple with kids. Orange Hair is reading an *Us Weekly*. In back it's incense and greeting cards. I slip the good book down my pants. My jacket obscures it. Easy peasy. I walk right out. Orange Hair doesn't even look up from her gossip.

Out in the mall, I'm in the food court. I flip it open—random page.

"What causes quarrels and causes fights among you? Is it not this, that your passions are at war within you? Do you not know that friendship with the world is enmity with God? Therefore whoever wishes to be a friend of the world makes himself an enemy of God."

Shit, man. Think.

I walk through the crowds, still thinking. What am I doing with the life I've been given? I haven't done anything. It's not even about right or wrong. I know I won't mess around with this forever. But I should at least live well. With quality.

I duck into the candy store. Every mall has one. I bag up a bunch of my favorites and just fucking bolt. I got the Bible in one hand and a bag in the other. I can't go wrong. Except a kid in his candy cane outfit is behind me. I'm faster than him though, I can tell. If I just keep bolting he'll give up. So I'm weaving in and out, knocking bags away.

"Hey, asshole!" I speed up. The new shoes help, that little extra grip. I can feel my leg muscles twitch in ecstasy. I'm enjoying this. I turn my head and he's further back. I bolt into Macy's. I'm running faster than I've ever run before. Perfume. Ladies'. Men's. Upstairs. Juniors. Sportswear. Kitchen. Bathroom. Furniture. I duck behind an armoire and count. There's no way he's even on this floor, I think.

I count to a hundred and don't hear anybody. I slip into the bathroom. I stand on the toilet seat and eat my gummy worms and wait. Nothing. He lost me.

I wait ten more minutes and then walk out, still counting candy.

That's when I feel the two hands on my shoulder. Guy with bleached blond hair and a mean look. Looks like that Rutgers guy in that movie Mr. Gannon made us watch. The robot.

"You're in a world of trouble, asswipe."

I just freeze. I stand there and he stands there, his paws clutching me. I don't look up.

He has to be mall renta. Couldn't be Macy's. They wouldn't have enough dogs in the race.

"The time for thinking was yesterday," he says. "Where are your parents?"

"I'm nineteen," I say.

"Like I said, where are your parents?"

He jabs me in the back with his finger.

"Let's you and me go in the back."

I don't say anything about Chief. I don't say anything about anything. I have to eat that shit. I know it.

I said the Bible is mine—luckily I peeled off the sticker already. So it's a bag of candy. They can't do shit for that. But he writes me up anyway, hands me the pink copy. It's like I'm getting fired from life. It won't be anything, though. Judge won't even look at it, and I'll just have to suck up the court fees. That's it.

Ironic. I wasn't even doing anything and I get caught. I bet the Renta keeps the candy for his fat ass.

I don't tell chief, Ally, nobody. The less they know about everything the better. I'm done with this. It's just when.

So I lay low. For about a week I watch television and eat popcorn.

Chief asks where I've been.

"School."

"Some lame excuse, my friend."

Whenever somebody says "buddy" or "my friend" it means the exact opposite.

Rule #13 from Chief. Perfect your practice. He likes to twist things inside out, but the meaning is the same.

Ally looks at me.

He sends us back to the sporting goods. This time—golf balls. Nothing but as many golf balls as we can get. Back to the booster bags.

This time there's an old plain-clothes following us. Comb over. I see him right off and nudge Ally. We're looking at the golf balls, but this guy is eyeballing us like we're made of bacon.

"727," I say.

Code for abort operation. Rule #22—pick your battles.

So we walk in. We're in the back. I like checking out the "outdoor zone"—tents and kayaks and backpacks. They have a kayak. Ally and I get in it. She's up front, I'm in back. We take the paddles and we're rowing.

The plainclothes is just standing there. Picking at a scab or something.

It's the Mississippi and we're flowing down into the lowlands. Cranes are lifting off as we paddle. Cattails are bobbing along the shore. We wave to the guys fishing and the ladies in the powerboat. The sun is out and I ask Ally if she needs more sunscreen. I drink from the cool water. It's refreshing and endless. Her eyes in my eyes. I can see my reflection in each pupil.

We have a long way to go and our energy is boundless.

The Wrong Hotel

George Bishop

I was thinking someone slept poorly here
the night before as I pulled the bed sheets

back, dreaming of new ways to keep from
dreaming. In my drinking days such visions

weren't easy to come by, I rarely appeared,
keeping my good eye on the present as it

sat somewhere in the room staring at itself
like a dead star. I've never been able to wish

on anything other than that, so here I am
surrounded by the afterglow of stale tobacco

and bad booze, sleepless. I think I'll stay
another night, maybe see what the maid

is made of—after all, the desk clerk threw me
the keys like I'd been here before. Same floor,

same room, just the wrong hotel, different night—
someone checking out inside, empty rooms full

of new moons and old nightmares, the light
of sleep still too far away to make out a face.

THE WHITE CEILING

PAUL COLBY

He sat down on the bed, took out his phone, and texted her the room number. He figured it would take her about five minutes to walk from the newsstand down the block, make her way through the sliding glass door and across the lobby, high heels clattering on the marble tiles, then wait for the elevator and ride up to the sixth floor. Make it seven minutes if there were other passengers in the elevator getting off before the sixth floor. As he unlaced his shoes and slid them off, he surveyed the room one more time.

The wallpaper had been the chief source of interest when he first entered. It had a sepia background and a dull gold print in the shape of keys that might have unlocked jail cells or bank vaults in the 1850s. He liked that the print was something you could actually recognize, and yet it meant next to nothing. There was nothing objectionable about the rest of the room—a queen-sized bed; an antique dresser dominated by a large, incongruous flat-screen TV; a breakfast table and two chairs, same color as the dresser but in a modern style. The carpet was a shade of beige that didn't even register as a color.

He only now noticed how white the ceiling was. With the room's other washed-out tones, you might have expected the whiteness to blend in, but it didn't. It shouted. It was a blankness that made you blink at first glance. But he decided that the room would do. It would serve their purposes, whatever they might turn out to be.

About two hours earlier they had closed on some land that her widowed father had deeded to the two of them while they were still married; the property had been divided into two lots as part of the divorce settlement, then recombined on the advice of a real estate agent when they opted to sell it to finance their son Ethan's four-year tuition at Davidson College. Immediately after shaking hands with the new owners, and the agent, and both teams of attorneys, they had decided to spend a little of the money on a on a celebratory meal at La Neige.

The dining room was mostly empty, making the meal seem like a strangely public experience. They imagined that the other diners, a pair of older women in one far corner, an underdressed threesome in another, could hear every clink of their silverware, every errant slurp as they sipped their wine. They spoke almost in whispers, giggling at themselves for their cloak-and-dagger discretion.

As they deliberated over whether to order a dessert, holding the leather-bound menu between them, he glanced at her averted face, admiring the way her new glasses concentrated the sharpness of her eyes; as if to heighten the appeal, she shifted in her chair just then, making her textured hose whisper ever so slightly.

"I've got a better idea," he said suddenly. "Beats the hell out of mousse."

She leaned back in her seat, a little slow to react but not displeased at all. "Why, you naughty boy. I guess I ought to be shocked."

"And yet you're not. Interesting."

"You're not talking about going back to your apartment, are you? Because if you mean my place..."

"I have to make an appearance at the office later, so no. Someplace close. I think I have just the right hotel in mind. You know the Daulton House?"

"Oh, God. Haven't they torn that place down yet?"

"No. Recently renovated, as a matter of fact. And very discreet, I understand."

"This is so funny, though. I mean, we don't have any luggage."

"I'll just say that the airline lost it."

"That's what everyone says, isn't it?"

"Yes. The hotel clerks are used to it. It's all part of the game."

"But they'll think we're having an affair. Kind of embarrassing." She blushed. In the twenty-two years he had known her, he'd never seen that happen, oddly enough. "Couldn't you buy a suitcase? You could always use an extra one, right?"

"And when the bellboy lifts it and there's nothing in it... Well, you let me register and then come in by yourself. Maybe they won't catch on."

As he sat on the edge of the bed now, patting the coverlet impatiently, he heard her knock at the door. Three quick knocks, a pause, then two slow ones. It was the signal they had laughingly agreed on.

When he opened the door, he found she had freshened her makeup and had taken the clip out of her hair; a little brushing had given it a fuller, thicker look, even making it slightly darker. He waited at the threshold, thinking they might kiss before she entered. She hesitated for a moment as if the same thing had crossed her mind, but then she abruptly rushed past him, taking in her surroundings as she entered the room.

"My God!" she said. "What a white ceiling!"

"Funny. I just noticed it myself. It *is* kind of white, isn't it?"

"I didn't know white could be so garish. They must have just painted it." She sniffed. "I don't smell fresh paint. But whoever was in this room this morning was having her period."

"You can smell that?"

She walked over to the wastebasket next to the dresser and peered into it. "They must have just taken out the trash."

"Really? Someone would throw it away in here?"

"A woman traveling alone... Sure."

"I could always get another room. This was the third one I looked at."

"So you shopped around?"

"I showed up without any luggage, remember? The desk clerk knew what I wanted the room for. He wasn't going to quibble if I was picky about it. He knew very well they'd be able to book it again tonight."

She dropped her purse down on the dresser, then leaned down to examine the ornate design. She ran her fingers along the molding, and tapped the top surface with the ends of her nails.

"Not bad, really," she said. "This is genuine teak. What was wrong with the other two rooms?"

"Something about them reminded me of places we've been already. Bad vibes, really. The first room made me think about that place where we stayed in New Orleans. When we were with the Sanderlings. You know, Keith was missing for about eighteen hours and turns out he was with that woman he knew from J. Walter Thompson, back in the nineties. Not exactly a good time, if you recall. The beginning of the end for them. And that's when things started going bad for us, too. It's like we caught the bug."

She had wandered to the window and opened the drapes, and was now gazing across the street at a freight truck that was being unloaded at the furniture store.

"It wasn't like that," she said, still gazing out the window. "What happened to us just happened. It's not something you can catch from someone else."

"Well, anyway. The wallpaper had the same color scheme. And then the other room... I hated it as soon as I walked in. Remember when we lived in Lubbock? Remember the neighbors?"

"Ugh." She turned away from the window and sat down on the bed. "I remember the way the water tasted. And it was so flat."

"It was mainly the things the neighbors used to say. And the kids. Christine used to come home with bruises on her arms from the little bitches on the bus. I was so glad when they transferred me after just a year. Thank God for that."

"We didn't have any wallpaper in that house."

"I know. It made me think of the sky. Blue with white flecks like cotton floating in the air. Even the sky was boring there."

"So you're turned off by wallpaper? And you didn't remember *this* print?" She was looking at the wall across from the end of the bed, her chin cupped in the spread fingers of her right hand, a wry smile on her face.

"What do you mean?"

"I mean, look at it. You don't remember seeing this design before?"

"Should I?" He studied it now for the third or fourth time, and a faint memory began to awaken. "Was it..."

"The committee room at Citizens Trust. Where we used to go for staff meetings. Before we started dating. Amazing you didn't see it."

A cheap shot, he thought, grinding his teeth slightly. According to her, he never noticed the important things, he was so involved in the small number of things that mattered to him, mainly the sorts of things that could be captured in decimals and percentages. According to her, anyway. Why would she suddenly need to give the knife one more turn?

"Should I change rooms again?" he asked in a flat voice.

"God, no. We didn't come here to look at the wallpaper. At least I didn't."

She rose from the bed and, without another word, slipped off her pumps, one after the other. She had the air of someone doing something practical and necessary, and there was something self-consciously blasé about her movements. In spite of that, and in spite of his irritation, she immediately had his full attention. There had always been something exciting to him about the sight of a woman in a skirt—especially a black, pleated skirt—taking off or putting on high-heeled shoes.

When she untucked her blouse from the waistband of her skirt and began unbuttoning it, his first thought was that she was going too fast. There were supposed to be some preliminaries, he imagined. She shouldn't be quite *this* practical. But instead of protesting, he watched, his heart beating a little faster with the undoing of each button and the gradual unveiling of her cranberry-red bra.

With one button to go, she stopped and looked at him. "What are you staring at? Is this a girlie show or something? Is that why we came up here?"

He smiled shyly. "Well, I guess I was doing it to you in my head down in the restaurant. That's probably what started it all."

"For the love of St. Peter," she said. "We were married for seventeen years. Didn't you get enough of it then? How long does it take you guys to grow up?"

"It's just part of the fun, isn't it? You get to watch me, too."

"Well, I don't feel like being stared at." She clasped her blouse shut, then went back to the window and yanked the cord to shut the drapes. Turning again, she strode barefoot across the room, snatching up her purse as she walked by the dresser. Reaching for the bathroom door, she said, "I'm going to undress in private, if you don't mind."

Once she closed the door, he shrugged to himself. He sat down on the nearest corner of the bed and began loosening his tie. His arousal, once sparked, continued to simmer, and as he undid his own buttons, he worked as quietly as possible, straining for the sounds of her clothes being removed. He distinctly heard the sound of a skirt placket being unfastened, heard the zipper, heard the fabric sliding down her legs, and as he listened he began to detect, or imagined he detected, the menstrual smell in the room. He was at half-mast before a full minute had gone by, making it difficult for him to unzip his trousers.

She remained in the bathroom longer than her disrobing required. How she passed the time until she came out was a mystery, but women's doings in bathrooms were always a mystery to him. No doubt the hotel had provided things for her to primp, deodorize, sterilize, depilate, or otherwise improve herself in some way. She had the resources of her ample purse, her tweezers, compact, nail file. And she could always improvise with plain water, a little saliva, and her fingers.

He was naked, sitting on the bed with his hands between his knees, still visibly aroused, when she finally came out of the bedroom, clutching a very large white commercial-grade towel to her chest, covering most of the front half of her body.

"Is that the last of the seven veils?" he asked her.

"I just decided that I'm not quite ready to be seen," she said, looking slightly askance, squinting near-sightedly in the absence of her glasses. "It's been at least three years."

"You mean since we made love or since I saw you without any clothes on?"

"Oh, don't even ask about making love. It's too depressing. We just gave up there at the end."

"You must have some good memories. Otherwise, why would you be here?"

"I'm overdue. That's why."

"So things haven't been so good between you and the piano salesman."

"His name is Burt, as if you didn't know, and that's been over for quite a while."

"But you're still on the pill?"

"Hope springs eternal. Yes, I am."

"I'm relieved to hear that."

He actually was relieved to know that all of the messy details had been taken care of. Perversely, though, the very mention of birth control was depressing. He saw no reason why it should be, but it was. He was losing his desire. As if to resist his failing passion, he stood up and approached her, and she got a good look at him in the state of nature.

"You've gained about ten pounds, haven't you?"

"Not ten. More like five. But thanks for noticing."

Her eyes settled on the middle of his body, and another wry smile appeared. He looked down at his stomach and his chest, and he was suddenly, shamefully aware of his pointed breasts and sagging belly. His waning desire was completely gone in an instant.

"No fair," he said glumly. "You got to see me. When do I get my turn?"

"I told you. I decided I'm not ready." She spread the towel wider across her shoulders. As usual, it was up to him to decipher her sudden shyness. Even though he was the one who was supposedly self-involved, she was the one who would fold her motives within her like words in an over-creased letter, then mock him when he wasn't able to make them out.

"Besides," she added, "you've seen it all."

"Not lately."

"Nothing's changed."

"Then drop the towel."

"No."

"Then put your goddamn clothes back on. We could just watch a dirty movie, if that's all you're in the mood for."

"That's not the worst idea."

"Good, then we can fantasize about doing unspeakable things to each other. I've got a few ideas already—movie or no movie."

At that moment, he actually had every intention of turning on the TV. Now that he was already in a state of abasement, every lump of flesh hanging out, he wondered what it would be like to expose himself to the dark-eyed, pregnant forecaster on the Weather Channel. He had already turned in the direction of the dresser when five sharp knocks on the door suddenly broke the thick tension in the room.

"Sorry to bother you, sir," a loud peremptory voice called out, sounding anything but apologetic. "Bell service."

"You didn't put out the Do Not Disturb sign," she whispered harshly.

"Didn't think about it."

Three more knocks. "Bell service, sir."

"I'll have to go to the door. He thinks I cheated him because I didn't have any luggage. He's not going to just go away."

He walked over to where his pants were lying on the floor, picked them up, and put them on, dispensing with underwear.

As he was half-dressing, he could see that she was clearly of two minds. For a second, she glanced toward the bathroom door; doing a quick about-face, she tip-toed across to the front corner of the room where his coat was hanging in a recessed nook. Drawing her shoulders together, she nestled to the right of the door hinges, where she was screened from view when he swung the door open

On the other side of the threshold was a man in gray slacks, a gray vest, and a black bow tie, a short man whose military bearing almost made him seem tall.

"Are you satisfied with your room, sir?" the man asked in a cold voice.

"Um. Yes. Quite satisfied."

"I'm glad to hear that, sir. Your luggage still hasn't arrived." The man very distinctly cleared his throat as soon as he had said this.

"No. Well, I'm sure the airline will send it right along."

"I'm sure," said the man in the vest, clearing his throat again, holding himself a little stiffer.

"Well..." He was conscious that she was standing not three feet away from him, not three feet away from the fully dressed man with the stern voice, who embodied some pretense of authority, and she was as naked as Eve, except for the towel. Her vulnerability was more erotic than anything he would have found on the dirty movie channel. It wasn't just the thought of her nude body, but the fact that she had made a deliberate decision to play a hiding game. He had a quick vision of her cool, erect nipples, and he was suddenly eager to get rid of the man before his own arousal became too embarrassingly obvious.

"Sir, is there anything—"

"Here, just...here." He reached back, almost surprised to find his wallet exactly where it was supposed to be, in his back pocket. He took out a five-dollar bill and placed it in the man's outstretched hand.

The man regarded the bill with faint distaste. "I'll be more than willing to call the airline for you."

"You do that. No need to come back until the bags arrive."

He shut the door a little too hard, then smiled irrepressibly when he saw her standing in the corner, clutching the towel tightly, rubbing her legs together.

"Close call," she said.

"He was no match for me."

"Huh. He got something for nothing, didn't he?"

He hadn't lost his new arousal, but he found himself becoming irritated with her again. The game she was playing was seemingly for her own amusement; his pleasure was beside the point. He felt that she wasn't giving him much of an opening, game or no game, clothes or no clothes. He began to wonder what she was doing here, flaying him with her archness and irony and concealment. For that matter, what were either of them were doing in this sterile, overpriced, stupidly decorated hotel room?

He decided that if there were any way of salvaging their splendid notion, it would have to begin with a kiss. So he stepped toward her, took hold of her bare shoulders, and leaned in with parted lips. She leaned forward slightly, just enough to allow her lips to make contact with his. Her lips felt a little coarse beneath the coating of dry lipstick, and when the two of them leaned back, he sensed that there had been no yielding at all. Merely the fact that he had kissed her, and that she returned his kiss in her own tentative fashion, suggested that something could be yielded, and might yet be.

She gave him a bemused look, then glanced down at her toes and wriggled them. He peered down, too, for the first time noticing that her toenails were painted cranberry-red, the same color as her bra. He wondered if her panties, wadded on the bathroom floor now, were the same color. He felt an added twinge of desire.

Suddenly she turned away from him and began walking across the room, padding over the carpet on flat arches.

"I think we missed our moment, that's all," she said, with a slight hitch in her voice.

"What do you mean 'our moment,'?" he asked petulantly.

She turned to face him. "Just that. We missed our moment. Just what I said."

"Do you mean now or then?"

Did she really mean—could she really mean—that their moment was five years ago, when he applied for that job with Morgan Stanley in New York, and they had gone window shopping for homes in Connecticut, happening upon the most perfect sixty-year-old house in a setting of maples and white fences? Did she mean that the right life for them was the one they all imagined, the two of them, and Christine and Ethan—that opalescent life of quiet evenings amid the sound of invisible doves, and fast, noisy weekend afternoons in the city, and the beaded lights across the bridges, and publishing firms where she could find an editing job, and a beach house on Long Island Sound, and antique shops, and community theater, and Coney Island? And did she mean that when, against all their realistic hopes, after four interviews and two ecstatic family trips to Manhattan, he lost out on the job, somehow the life that was meant for them had receded into the nether land of interrupted dreams?

"What difference does it make, now or then?" she said, her voice getting harder with every word she spoke.

"It makes a difference to me. You're making it sound as if I did something wrong."

She sighed and shook her head at him. "Right. So it always depended on you. As if there weren't things that I could have done differently."

He expected her to disappear into the bathroom, and she might have, if he had said anything else. But he held his tongue and waited to see what she would decide to do. There was a pained look in her eyes as she surveyed the room from wall to wall again, contemplating those rows of matching keys, meant to fasten a thousand locks, then glancing up at the unbearably white ceiling.

"I really don't feel like putting my clothes back on," she said. "It's almost too much of an effort. Manual labor."

Making her way across the carpet, she dodged the breakfast table and walked over to the far side of the bed, close to the window, where green-tinted light was coming in through the drapes.

"I think I just want to lie here for a little while. You can do what you want to do."

She let the towel drop down to the floor, stretched out on the coverlet, flat on her back, and closed her eyes.

So she was forcing him to read her motives again, he thought. Was her complete nakedness now a gesture of disdain, as if it didn't matter to her whether he could see her or not? Or was it an invitation? Since her eyes were closed anyway, he felt no inhibition about approaching her and looking more closely.

Her proportions hadn't changed in any way that he could see. Nothing surprised him, in any case. Her breasts were neither larger nor smaller than he remembered. Right now they spread across her chest like a very thick liquid, crested by pebbly nipples. Her flesh was pooled along the undersides of her breasts and around her navel, and along her hip bones. Her thighs were scored by well-remembered stretch marks and ripples of fat, but below her knees her muscles were still very well-defined.

From outside the window, beyond the closed drapes, he could hear the furniture movers yelling instructions and curses at each other.

After flicking off the lamp on the nightstand next to the dresser, he slipped out of his trousers and lay down on the bed next to her. The voices in the street below almost seemed louder now. Drivers were honking their horns as they tried to get past the truck. The workday sounds made it seem as if there were something wrong in lying there, unclothed, as the business of the world was transacted just beyond two pieces of fabric and one thin pane of glass. Something wrong, or at least something different. If they ended up making love now, at this time of day, in this utterly strange place, it would be a different kind of experience.

He glanced to the side and found that she now had her eyes open. He checked his brief impulse to speak, once again deciding that silence would serve him better.

The fear that now took hold of him was the product of failure. Seventeen failed years of marriage. So much that was good blotted out by so much that was wrong. As he stared again at the white ceiling he swallowed hard. Hesitating for a moment, because of that fear, he reached over blindly and found her bent elbow, then slid his fingers down her arm until he found her hand; he lay still, staring at the ceiling, as she responded by clasping his hand.

"My God!" he heard her say. "Even with the light off and drapes closed, it's just as white as it can be! I feel like I'm going snow blind."

That blankness was forbidding but also strangely inviting. It was something you could fall into, he imagined. Something deep, without end.

NANU NANU

JIM GUSTAFSON

for Robin Williams

Listen to you
shake your heads
rattle your thoughts crazy,
pretending you have no idea
why a funny man would take
his breath away.

Laughter is the voice of tears,
a smile the scar of a thin blade.
Beneath smooth green lawns
the soil is always dark.
It cannot stand up to the light.
The weeds weep this night.

Ol' Sally

Keith Stahl

That boy Dashawn towered in front of Walter's car, middle of Arbor Drive, bouncing his basketball like an African drum. The gallows leaned into the street: rusty, portable hoop with cracked backboard and frayed net dangling from one string. Walter clearly signaled the left turn into his own driveway, but didn't lay on the horn or make eye contact. Dashawn wanted that; that was the game: feign oblivion and make The Man wait. Walter's white hair made him a bullseye for polar bear hunters playing the knockout game (he read the news), and the last thing he needed was a gang of Dashawns looking to blindside him one night in the Walmart parking lot. Blast the thawing Hungry Man dinners and Neapolitan ice cream in the trunk of his Buick. Walter had all day.

He inched closer, bumper almost nudging Dashawn from behind.

Dashawn dribbled, eyes closed, Red Bull in his free hand, head bobbing side to side like a cobra, rapping out loud over his head phones, "My chain heavy, yeah, yeah, my chain heavy, my chain heavy, my chain too heavy."

Walter turned up Glenn Beck.

Dashawn tilted his head like a Pez, downed his energy drink, ambled to the curb.

This was Walter's chance. But he had to wait for a Rent-a-Center truck.

Dashawn deposited the empty Red Bull into the knot of the Norway maple in Walter's yard.

Walter strangled his steering wheel. He lurched into the driveway. Spinning tires spit crumbling asphalt.

He wanted to spring from his car and rip that can from Ol' Sally's knot and shove it in Dashawn's thirteen-year-old face: "Lose this?" If the city of Syracuse finally got around to sending the Rick Turk Tree Service to cut down Ol' Sally, garbage from the neighborhood "kids" would spill from her trunk like that scene from *Jaws*. Doritos bags and crushed Newport packs and a spent Chivas Regal. Empty 40s.

But the neighborhood was no longer carpeted bluegrass and Geranium window boxes and manicured yew. It was flaking bungalows, buckling sidewalks, foot-long grass gone to seed. Shrubs flirted with roofs. Grass tufts sprang from driveway cracks like the Brillo in Walter's ears.

And it wasn't like Helen and Walter's initials were carved into the bark. There was no wise, old face if you looked at the knots right. Walter never hung a tire swing from the branches, never watched with Helen from the porch as Kimberly pushed her little brother Kevin higher and higher in the swing that was never there. It wasn't third base for stick ball games. It wasn't the home for any particular family of robins. Walter didn't fill the tree with cobwebs at Halloween, didn't hide with Helen as the giant spider he never rigged dropped onto trick-or-treaters. The family never rolled in a pile of raked leaves, teasingly calling for Bess, the dog who yipped and danced and howled for them to get out of there. Walter never hung Christmas lights to outdo the neighbors, never hung Easter eggs or American flags or yellow ribbons. There was no tree house.

Walter never even called the tree "Ol' Sally" until the day he stood on his porch and read the notification that the Norway maple was condemned. He never knew it was called a *Norway maple*. So it wasn't like when the Rick Turk Tree Service came, Walter was planning to chain himself to the tree with that old bicycle lock from the basement and swallow the key. His arms weren't going to chafe and burn, wrapped around the trunk, splinters in his face, spitting bark, swarming black ants. He wasn't going to contact Greenpeace, or get himself arrested, or wave around a shot gun and commit suicide-by-cop. There'd be no throwing himself under the trucks, or dousing himself with gasoline and lighting a match, or climbing the tree to jump into the chipper, or beheading of the Rick Turk Tree Service guys with their own chainsaws, "LA LA LA LA LA"—while teen mothers circled their strollers, yelled into cell phones, "Man, that's dope!"

It was out of Walter's wrinkled hands. According to the city of Syracuse, the tree was unbalanced and structurally unsound, and it was fascist policy to maintain a safe and healthy tree population. They didn't say when. The red "ASAP" implied the tree might fall down before it was cut down, and every morning Walter braced himself to find Ol' Sally sprawled in the yard. Arbor Drive was the death row of trees. Maybe Dashawn's Red Bull can was Ol' Sally's last meal.

"My chain heavy, yeah, yeah, my chain heavy, my chain heavy, my chain too heavy."

Walter heard it over Glenn Beck, even though he'd gone deaf in one ear—half-blind, too, from his pregnant mother contracting rubella. Walter heard everything in the neighborhood over anything else, even in the house. He was an idiot savant. It was a curse. Rap music over his white noise machine, the guttural bark of pit bulls over Barbra Streisand, the shattering cry of Dashawn's grandmother—"DAY-SHAWN!"—over *Cops Reloaded.*

He'd probably hear Dashawn's grandmother later, whooping him for missing school again. That wouldn't be so bad.

Walter had never skipped school, and his half-deafness and half-blindness never stopped him, back in the day, from working seventy hours a week. He paid taxes so Dashawn would have a school to skip. He paid for the new Section Eight housing at the end of the street. Walter paid off the mortgage three years early, and there was always cash (never credit) for Helen when she walked the kids to Sears on Salina Street on Saturdays, Kimberly toddling in that white, English cotton party dress while she pushed her baby brother's stroller, stopping to smell the Schultz's roses, Helen waving to Bob Johnson, perpetually troweling dandelions across the street: "The American dream, eh Bob?" Not that Walter ever got to join his family for those shady strolls. He worked Saturdays. Somebody had to work Saturdays.

Terrorists rented the Schultz's next door. Cell phones, backpacks, hijab. At least they were quiet neighbors.

Bob Johnson left, replaced at first by a family missing a lot of teeth who parked their truck on Bob Johnson's old dandelions. Then the Dashawns.

They boarded up Sears on Salina Street forty years ago, sold the building to an out-of-towner for one dollar.

It wasn't long after Sears that Walter explained the U-Haul in the driveway to Bob Johnson— "It's a good thing, a positive thing, all very amicable"—while Helen's friends solemnly carried out half the furniture, half the dishes, half the books. Walter would still see the kids, once in a while. He even helped the movers disassemble Kevin's crib. (Where had Helen met all these people?

Night school? Martial Arts?) He smirked at Bob Johnson, "What a way to celebrate the Bicentennial." He admitted to Bob Johnson he was looking forward to walking around the house naked. (He told Bob Johnson don't worry. He told Bob Johnson he'd close the curtains.)

After Helen's U-Haul left, Walter discovered things. He called Helen and asked if she had meant to leave Bess' dog food. Had she simply forgotten the Kodak in the kitchen drawer?

She said he was being *manipulative*.

Walter invited everybody for Thanksgiving years later, and Helen said the same thing. *Manipulative*. Walter wanted to fill the empty Kodak with group shots of Helen and her new husband, What's-His-Name, and their baby boy and Kimberly and Kevin and all those grandkids. He'd take pictures of Helen's pies, pictures of Kevin's five-year-old coming to terms with a drumstick bigger than his head.

Manipulative.

Kimberly and Kevin were busy with work, anyway. And Walter was clueless how to cook a turkey.

"My chain heavy, yeah, yeah, my chain heavy, my chain heavy, my chain too heavy."

Dashawn pulled at his crotch like a holstered gun, cradled the basketball against his hip. He couldn't be oblivious to Walter, even with the headphones and the dark sunglasses and the crooked Yankee cap. Dashawn was deliberate, absolutely one hundred percent deliberate. This was all about White Privilege. This was all about White Flight. This was all about Racial Profiling. Reparations. Whatever. Dashawn pulled his junk out and urinated on Ol' Sal.

Walter turned off the car. He struggled with the seat belt, arthritic hands trembling like tectonic plates. His back popped like bubble-wrap, but he got out. He straightened up to his full five feet, seven inches. He adjusted his pants, came around the car with his hands on his belt. He sauntered across the yard like it was the OK Corral.

Dashawn swiveled his head and hopped. "Oh, snap!" He dropped the basketball to Walter's lawn with a muffled *ping ping ping*. Dashawn tucked away his penis with both hands, frantic, dribbled a little in his pants.

Walter trembled. Walter dribbled a little in his own pants.

Dashawn backed into the street. He abandoned the basketball, turned and sprinted to his grandmother's house. He slammed his front door. It echoed like a bomb. The glitchy storm door that Bob Johnson installed fifty years before creaked open with the retort.

Dashawn's urine stained Ol' Sally's bark. Yellow foam pooled in the grass. His Red Bull can shone like a coat of arms, teetering atop a crumpled KFC bag in Ol' Sally's knot. Walter drew it out, studied the can like divorce papers. Then he hurled it across the street into Dashawn's yard.

Dashawn's mini-blinds moved. Walter furiously kicked at the basketball, grazing the top, straining his hamstring. The ball rolled feebly across the street and settled against the curb. Walter was a superhero, fists on hips. "Game on," he wheezed.

Walter yanked refuse from the knot like a magician pulls flowers from his sleeve. One hand at first, then two. He found a rhythm, like Helen's tai chi, or whatever she was doing back in the day. Feminism. He showered the neighborhood with McFlurry cups and Thank You bags. He didn't care what he touched. He was old. We're all going to get something, someday. Ebola. Aids. Whatever. Wet Kleenex trickled from Ol' Sally's knot like vomit. There were Styrofoam boxes and chicken bones, a broken Captain America and Band-Aids, used condoms and graded homework. The garbage accumulated like snow.

Walter's knuckles bled. He scraped his forearms and elbows. His heart sounded like crashing waves in his head. There was more garbage in Ol' Sally's trunk, but it was down too deep. He wished he could climb into the knot like a squirrel. He'd curl up and die. They'd take him away when they came for Ol' Sally, wouldn't even know he was there.

He limped into the house with his groceries.

Walter stacked Campbell's Soups against yellowing cans of Alpo in the cupboard. The cans began to vibrate like chattering teeth. Walter thought of 9/11. The house shook. Maybe it was surrounded by armored vehicles, tanks. He moved to the living room window, expecting a war zone.

They were fast and sudden, like a drug bust. Three thundering trucks to tackle Ol' Sal: The Picker, The Chipper, The Claw. Five men stood in orange hard hats, red ear muffs, and lime-green Day-Glo T-shirts. They wanted to be seen, but hid their eyes behind dark sunglasses.

On one of the trucks, Ol' Sally's branches partially blocked "Rick Turk Tree Service." It looked like "Fuck Fuck."

This was it. These were Ol' Sally's final moments.

There was a presence up there. Walter couldn't see the man high up in The Picker from the window, but the chainsaw whirred and leaf-filled branches fell like confetti. The Chipper smote wood to sawdust, trilled like a dentist's drill. The Claw wheeled, farted hydraulics, vise-gripped the tree's thick limbs and fed them to The Chipper. It growled in ecstasy. Exhaust tasted like expired cans of soup. The Claw stabbed the hundred-year-old trunk. Without branches, it looked like a peace sign. A chainsaw sliced through the jugular. The Claw lifted the trunk. It swung like a corpse. The Chipper swallowed hard and Ol' Sally was gone.

Helen and Walter never sat on the porch in the shade of Ol' Sally on warm summer days, sipping lemonade, as Kimberly and Kevin counted for Hide-and-Seek with their faces buried in Ol' Sally's trunk. Walter never sat out with his wife at night with the lights out, chamomile tea, storm moving in, kids snoring preciously in their beds, wind swooshing Ol' Sally's canopy while rain ticked her leaves like a metronome. Helen never jumped onto Walter's lap, giddy at the booming thunder, wet from the bursting deluge, eyes flashing in the lightning, "Let's take our clothes off." But Walter thought he should have taken pictures. The Kodak had all that unused film. He could have taken a "before" shot of Ol' Sally, and an "after" shot of the empty space. Maybe sent the pictures to Helen.

Or was that *manipulative*?

The men raked the remaining leaves and twigs from Walter's yard. They cleared sawdust from the sidewalk with gas-powered leaf blowers.

The garbage. Piles of exposed evidence. Had anyone seen him? Dashawn had seen him. They'd shackle Walter, haul him to the Justice Center, throw him in a cage. Was it technically Walter's garbage? He wasn't about to clean up somebody else's mess while Dashawn gloated over him like an elementary school principal. He'd drag Dashawn down with him. He'd find that Red Bull can. They'd take fingerprints. Dashawn started it.

It was during *Jeopardy*. That voice, like revving chainsaws, drew Walter back to his window. Dashawn's grandmother discovered the boy had skipped school. She was leaving for her night job, and when she got back, she didn't care whose it was, that garbage had to be picked up.

All of it.

She was a fat angel in her starched, white uniform. The ghost of Ol' Sally. She waddled toward the bus stop.

Dashawn shook his head like a neighing horse. He wrestled on yellow dish gloves. He snapped open a Hefty bag, bent over, and dangled his long arm to the ground. He lifted an Oreo wrapper. It was like a heavy brick. He forced it to the bottom of the trash bag. He shuffled through the sea of Bob Johnson's old dandelions, dragging the bag behind him, slowly and methodically picking up garbage. When he fired heavier bottles and cans into the plastic bag, it sounded like whips.

Doubled over like that, Dashawn resembled Bob Johnson. Walter had stood at this very window one Sunday, laughing at Bob Johnson flailing away at his lawn mower. Bob Johnson yanked the cord so hard his arm would pop out. It was spark plugs. Walter had a box full. He had Bob Johnson's mower going in no time.

But Walter wasn't about to get clocked on the head, kicked in the face, stomped on. He wasn't going to don his cardigan and step into the chill September evening with his trash bag and his garden gloves. He wasn't going to death-grip the handrail and shuffle down those porch steps, knees crackling like fireworks. He wasn't about to squat to the curb and start picking up the garbage.

So Dashawn would never grin like a Cheshire cat, cross from his side of the street to put the empty Red Bull can into Walter's trash bag. The two would never silently fill their trash bags with generations of garbage as the street lights came on. It wasn't like Dashawn would give Walter a hand up when it was done.

Where Are You, Gravity?

Patricia Colleen Murphy

—for Nick Flynn

This house is a bridge for sale, a poker game, a firefly. It's a time warp, a time machine, a trap. It's worker's comp, rehab, restitution, order to re-convey. This house is a big sick lung. This house is a cave, a hovel, a hole. In this house we found everything that was lost. Two necklaces—one jade, one lapis; the land, the water. Shirt in a drawer for 35 years. This house is a 35-years drawer.

When he said, "You cannot come home." I said, "As you wish." I made a little house in my head. For five years, every phone call every letter. I pounded my chest. Gave five reasons why. Chanel N°5, size five shoes, five fingers, five toes, five little wishes. Five times with love or humility. Five times I left all I had on the begging table.

I'm arriving late for the party. I hear my father shuffling a plastic shopping bag. I hear him coughing like a symphony—strings, horns, percussion, brass. I try, but I can't hold my own breath as long as that cough.

Where are you, gravity? The first time I asked I was so pure that if you touched me I would shatter. The first time I asked he said shock treatments, Thorazine, Lithium, restraints. The first time I asked, I wished I could be the bad child, the semi-conscious, the fat.

I wished I had never seen her thumb and its pulse. A thumb like a snake's head, like a dying thing. Like a crooked branch, like a fidgeting foot. A thumb that swaggers, accelerates, circles, flexes, points, taps, pounds, pouts, pleads, pinches. A thumb that wrestles itself. A thumb hitching a bad ride. A thumb being sucked. A thumb in the crack of the dam.

Where are you, gravity? When I tell my father never to die but he knows he is already dying? Packing to race to his deathbed feels like a goddamn Sharon Olds poem. The distance was the sanity in the first place. I wanted to open that door and find my mother and father at my age. Where are you, gravity? Where are you when the spinning-spasm starts? Where are you when the spinning-spasm ends?

CONTRIBUTOR NOTES

BARBARA ABRAMSON's fiction has appeared in *The Fiddlehead, The West Coast Review,* and *Waccamaw*.

MK AHN's writing has appeared in *Fence, Kori: Anthology of Korean American Fiction, The Adoption Reader,* and *Seeds from a Silent Tree.* A graduate of the Bennington Writing Seminars, she is currently working on a collection of short stories as well as a novel, and teaches at Ewha Women's University in Seoul, Korea.

GEORGE BISHOP's work has appeared in *Carolina Quarterly & Lindenwood Review.* Forthcoming work will be featured in *Pirene's Fountain.* He is the author of seven chapbooks. Bishop won the 2013 Peter Meinke Prize at YellowJacket Press for his chapbook, *Following Myself Home,* and was a 2014 Pushcart Prize nominee. He attended Rutgers University and now lives in Saint Cloud, FL.

G. DAVIS CATHCART is an illustrator currently residing in Ridgewood Queens, New York City. He has studied art and illustration at the Cooper Union, Maryland Institute College of Art, and Rhode Island School of Design, where he graduated in 2012. He has worked for Maira Kalman, William Wegman, and *The New Yorker*'s art department. Davis currently teaches art to children of all ages in public schools all over New York City. Both RISD and the Society of Illustrators have given him awards for his illustration work. The work represented here is often described as a study on childhood, usually boyish but always depicted tenderly, overloaded with nostalgia. Even when dealing with aggressive subjects, these illustrations place an emphasis on discovery, adventure, and exploring new ground.

GEORGE L. CHIEFFET received an MFA from UNC-Greensboro, where he studied with Fred Chappell, Robert Watson, and other well-known Southern writers. George favors stories about marginalized people and his stories often reflect their predicaments. He has published stories in *Furnace, Greensboro Review, Per Contra, Barely South, storySouth*, and other journals. His story, "Love Valley," was selected among the 2011 *storySouth* Million Writers Award Notable Stories.

SAJA CHODOSH (Sage) recently graduated from Washington University in St. Louis with a degree in English Literature and Marketing. She was born in NYC, spent her childhood in Cleveland, her adolescence in Salt Lake City, and her college years between St. Louis, London, and her family's new home outside LA. This movement spurred her graviton with ideas of place, space, and home. Sage explores these themes in her writing, and is currently working on a poetry manuscript that aims to reconstruct home through words. She has been published in *Issues Magazine, Tigress Magazine for Girls,* and the *Nemerov Anthology : To The Forest.* You are invited to wander through her website, sajachodosh.com, as well as her blog, doorwaydance.com.

PAUL COLBY is a fiction writer and playwright currently moonlighting as a Professor of English at North Carolina State University. His stories have recently appeared in *SN Review* and *Pilcrow & Dagger*. Paul lives in rural Wake County, near Raleigh, with his wife Robin, his son Evan, and a blended family of possums and feral cats. He is at work on his fifth novel.

MARK CRIMMINS's fiction has been nominated for a 2015 Pushcart Prize, a 2015 Silver Pen Authors Association Write Well Award, and a 2014 Best of the Net Award. His short stories have been published in *Confrontation, Cha, Split Rock Review, Penmen Review, Trainless Magazine,*

Quarterly Literary Review Singapore, Kyoto Journal, and *Eclectica.* His flash fictions have been published in *Happy, theNewerYork, White Rabbit, Columbia* online, *Tampa Review Online, Eunoia Review, Flash Frontier, Portland Review, Pif, Gravel,* and *Eastlit.* He holds a PhD in Twentieth Century Literature from the University of Toronto and has been teaching Contemporary Fiction at the University of Toronto since 1999.

JESSICA CUELLO is a graduate of Barnard College who teaches French in Central NY. Her poems have appeared in *Copper Nickel, RHINO, Conte, Tampa Review,* and other journals. She has received two Best of the Net nominations and the 2010 Vivienne Haigh-Wood Prize. A chapbook of poems about Marie Curie is forthcoming from Kattywompus Press.

ANDIE FRANCIS is the author of the chapbook, *I Am Trying to Show You My Matchbook Collection* (CutBank 2015). Her work appears or is forthcoming in *Cimarron Review, CutBank, Fjords Review, Greensboro Review, Portland Review,* and *Timber.*

GLENN FREEMAN has published two collections of poetry, *Keeping the Tigers behind Us* and *Traveling Light.* He teaches writing and American literature at Cornell College in small-town Iowa, where he lives with his wife and two cats.

LAUREN GENOVESI's work has appeared in *Gulf Coast, Nerve, American Literary Review, Poet Lore,* and other magazines. A graduate of the Creative Writing Program at the University of Houston, she teaches at the Community College of Philadelphia and is at work on a collection of stories.

JIM GUSTAFSON teaches at Florida Gulf Coast University and Florida Southwestern State College, and holds an MFA from the University of Tampa. His chapbook, *Driving Home,* was published by Aldrich Press in 2013. Jim lives in Fort Myers, FL where he reads, writes, and pulls weeds. Visit him online at jimgustafson.com.

STEPHANIE RENAE JOHNSON is a freelance writer and editor living in the mountain town of Asheville, North Carolina. An avid lover of children's literature and poetry, she is working on her first young adult novel and poetry chapbook while pursuing her Masters in Writing at Lenoir-Rhyne University. Her work—poetry, nonfiction, and fiction—has been published by *Danse Macabre, Fat City Review, Prick of the Spindle,* and *Slink Chunk Press.*

RUDY KOSHAR lives in Madison, Wisconsin with his wife of more than forty years. His short fiction and nonfiction have appeared most recently in *Eclectica, Black Heart Magazine, Guernica, Montreal Review, Revolution House, Red Fez,* and *Turk's Head Review.* His awards include a Guggenheim fellowship and second place in the Wisconsin Academy of Sciences, Arts, & Letters' 2013 Fiction Contest. He teaches in the history department at the University of Wisconsin-Madison.

NATHAN LESLIE is the author of six books of short fiction, one book of poetry and editor of two anthologies. He is the fiction editor for *Pedestal Magazine* and was the series editor for Best of the Web. He lives in Northern Virginia and teaches at Northern Virginia Community College.

KRISTEN MACKENZIE lives on Vashon Island in a quiet cabin where the shelves are filled with herbs for medicine-making, the floor is open for dancing, and the table faces the ocean, waiting for a writer to pick up the pen. Her work has appeared in *Brevity, Rawboned Journal, GALA Magazine, Extract(s) Daily Dose of Lit,* and is included monthly in *Diversity Rules Magazine.* Pieces are forthcoming in *Blank Fiction, Crack the Spine Literary Magazine, Maudlin House, The Doctor T. J. Eckleburg Review, Wilderness House Journal, Bluestockings Magazine,* and *MadHat Annual.* Her short story, "Cold Comfort," placed as an Honorable Mention in The Women's National Book Association's annual writing contest and will be published in a special edition of the association's journal, *Bookwoman,* in June.

DERICK MATTERN has an MFA from the University of Wisconsin, Madison. His poems and translations have appeared or are forthcoming in *Copper Nickel, Subtropics, Gulf Coast, Whiskey Island*, and elsewhere.

PATRICIA COLLEEN MURPHY teaches creative writing at Arizona State University, where she is the founding editor of the literary magazine, *Superstition Review*. Her poems have appeared in many journals, including *The Iowa Review, Quarterly West, The American Poetry Review,* and most recently in *North American Review, Smartish Pace, Burnside Review, Poetry Northwest, Third Coast, Hobart, decomP, Midway Journal, Armchair/Shotgun, Natural Bridge,* and others. Her poems have received awards from *Glimmer Train* Press, *The Southern California Review, Gulf Coast, The Madison Review, Bellevue Literary Review*, and others. You can read more about her at patriciacolleenmurphy.com.

CALEB NELSON, originally from Montana, currently lives in the upper peninsula of Michigan. He is studying poetry in the Master of Fine Arts program at Northern Michigan University and is Associate Poetry Editor of *Passages North*.

CYNTHIA REESER is the founder and publisher of Aqueous Books, and founder and editor-in-chief of *Prick of the Spindle*. Cynthia earned a BA in English Literature from Arizona State University, an MFA in Creative Writing - Fiction from the University of Tampa, and attended the University of Oxford (Magdalen College), Oxford, UK as a Visiting Student; she also holds an AA in Piano Performance. She has published more than 100 reviews in print and online, as well as poetry and fiction in print and online. She is the author of the poetry chapbook, *Light and Trials of Light* (Finishing Line Press, 2010), and two books of reference from Atlantic Publishing. Her short stories are anthologized in the *Daughters of Icarus Anthology* (Pink Narcissus Press, 2013), and in *Follow the Blood: Tales Inspired by The Hardy Boys and Nancy Drew* (Sundog Lit, 2013). Cynthia recently completed a literary short story collection inspired by fairy tale lore. See her visual art online at cynthiareeser.com.

NATALIE SHARP's work has previously appeared in *The Peacock's Feet* and *Poemeleon: The Disobedient Issue*. She was also a 2013 finalist for the Margaret Harvin Wilson Writing Award. Natalie currently lives in Milledgeville, GA, where she is an avid participant in community workshops and local performance poetry events.

EVA SKRANDE's poems have appeared in *Alaska Quarterly, The Iowa Review, APR*, and many other magazines. Her book, *My Mother's Cuba*, was published in the *River City Poetry Series* by River City Publishing. She lives and teaches in Houston, TX.

KEITH STAHL's work has recently appeared in *The Madison Review, Ghost Town, Per Contra*, and *Corium*. Keith is a non-traditional undergraduate student pursuing a degree in English and Textual Studies on the Creative Writing Track at Syracuse University.

CARMEN K. WELSH, JR. (yes, she's a girl) holds an AA in Art Ed, a BSc in Web Design, and a newly-minted MFA in Creative Writing. She's published illustrations, short stories, and articles in fanzines, anthologies, e-zines, lit blogs, and two literary print journals. She's a member of the Association of Writers & Writing Programs, as well as a member of the Furry Writers' Guild. Two of her out-of-print fictions became podcasts (with background music and sound effects!). Her official website is http://TabbertheRed.com, named after her feline warrior character from the world her six published short stories are based in. You can find her bibliography on http://TheAngryGoblin.wordpress.com. Her ongoing art portfolio (with works old and new) can be found on CopperSphinx on DeviantArt.

PRICK OF THE SPINDLE

WE'VE (VIRTUALLY) MOVED! COME VISIT US ONLINE AT OUR NEW HOME:
WWW.PRICKOFTHESPINDLE.ORG

Where you can submit your work, find out more about us, and purchase needful things such as subscriptions, past issues, and ironic T-shirts.

And visit our new visual art galleries on the website, while you're at it! They are a treat to the senses. We also publish independent short film. Guidelines are online.

We are always looking for book reviewers. View our new online Book Reviews section and the Review Shelf, a listing of our currently available titles for reviewers, at http://prickofthespindle.org/reviewer-guidelines/

Prick of the Spindle is currently seeking humor columnists for The Corner, a new column on the website featuring satirical and edgy nonfiction pieces, quips, and cartoons. If interested, send clips to pseditor@prickofthespindle.com.

ISSN 1940-5499

Prick of the Spindle is a 501(c)(3) nonprofit organization.

PRICK OF THE SPINDLE
A JOURNAL OF THE LITERARY ARTS

CPSIA information can be obtained
at www.ICGtesting.com
Printed in the USA
LVOW02s1920230316
480468LV00004B/7/P